FIDEL CASTRO

Cuban Revolutionary **BY WARREN BROWN**

The
Millbrook
Press □
Brookfield,
Connecticut

Library of Congress Cataloging-in-Publication Data
Brown, Warren, 1963–
Fidel Castro : Cuban Revolutionary / by Warren Brown.
p.   cm.
Includes bibliographical references and index.
Summary: Describes the rise to power of the revolutionary leader
opposed to the corruption and violence of the Batista regime, and
the many strands of his more than thirty years of rule.
ISBN 1-56294-385-5 (lib. bdg.)
1. Castro, Fidel, 1927–   —Juvenile literature.   2. Cuba—
History—1959–   —Juvenile literature.   3. Heads of state—Cuba—
Biography—Juvenile literature.   4. Revolutionaries—Cuba—
Biography—Juvenile literature.   [1. Castro, Fidel, 1927–
2. Heads of state.   3. Cuba—History—1959–]   I. Title.
F1788.22.C3B76   1994
972.9106'4'092—dc20   [B]
93-25211   CIP   AC

Published by The Millbrook Press
2 Old New Milford Road, Brookfield, Connecticut 06804

Photos courtesy of AP/Wide World Photos: pp. 1,
38, 42, 53, 65, 70, 89, 112; UPI/Bettmann: pp. 6, 20,
35, 47, 62, 76, 78, 80, 94, 100, 102; The Bettmann
Archive: pp. 15, 17, 27, 56. Map by Frank Senyk.

Contents

FIDEL CASTRO

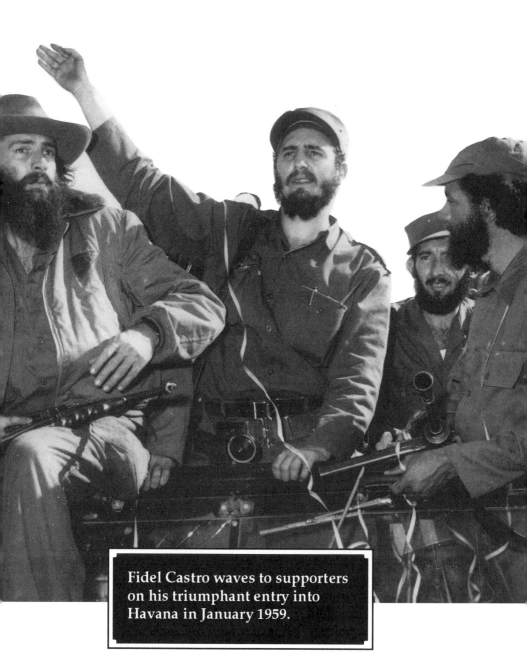

Fidel Castro waves to supporters on his triumphant entry into Havana in January 1959.

1

"You Are Doing All Right, Fidel!"

On Thursday afternoon, January 8, 1959, the residents of Havana, Cuba, flocked into the bright winter sunshine. Men, women, and children gathered by the hundreds of thousands, lining the streets and filling the balconies and rooftops of the island's capital city. Joy and excitement filled the air. The people of Havana had turned out to celebrate Cuba's freedom from two decades of dictatorship and to welcome their liberator, Fidel Castro.

At five minutes to three, the crowds near the Shrine of the Virgin of the Road, on the eastern outskirts of the city, cheered as a column of tanks, jeeps, and armored cars rumbled into view. Each vehicle carried dark-haired soldiers in dirty combat fatigues, many of whom sported luxuriant beards. These were the rebels of Castro's victorious 26th of July Movement, known affectionately in Cuba as *los barbudos*, "the bearded ones."[1]

The cheering rose to a fever pitch as the crowd caught sight of its idol. Castro, dressed in olive-green fatigues and wearing an army cap, sat atop a tank that had been recently "liberated" from the Cuban army. Looking exhausted but happy as he waved to the crowd, the thirty-two-year-old rebel leader towered above his companions, a cigar clenched between his teeth and a bushy black beard framing his round, youthful face. Next to him stood his nine-year-old son Fidelito ("little Fidel"), who had been sent to school in New York for his safety and brought back to Cuba after his father's victory.

As Castro rode toward the city's waterfront he was greeted by shouts of "¡Viva Castro!" from happy people waving the red, white, and blue flag of the Cuban Republic and the black and red flag of the 26th of July Movement. Church bells rang, factory whistles blew, and Cuban naval vessels in the harbor fired salutes.

CASTRO'S TRIUMPHANT ENTRY into Havana marked the end of a long and bitter odyssey. For more than two years the young lawyer-turned-revolutionary had battled the corrupt dictatorship of President Fulgencio Batista from the Sierra Maestra mountains, in Oriente Province at the southeastern end of the island. With the help of local peasants, he had built up a small but highly disciplined guerrilla force that outfought Batista's large, well-equipped army at every turn.

In the summer of 1958, after surviving a final attempt by Batista's demoralized men to dislodge him from the mountains, Castro launched a final offensive. Within months, hundreds of bearded rebels were sweeping through the eastern half of the island, capturing towns and military outposts daily and welcoming new recruits to their ranks. On New Year's Day, 1959, Batista fled with his family to the nearby Dominican Republic. He left behind an army of 46,000 men that had been defeated by two to three thousand rebels.

Castro reacted swiftly. Fearful that the commanders of Batista's army would take control of the government, he issued a call for a general strike. Workers responded by walking off their jobs in droves, shutting down the country and blocking an attempt by army officers to seize power. Castro then ordered two of his field commanders, Camilo Cienfuegos and Ernesto Guevara (known popularly as "Che") to take their men and occupy Havana.

On January 3, Castro set out for Havana himself from Santiago de Cuba, the capital of Oriente Province. The journey became a five-day celebration. Thousands lined the road to catch a glimpse of their hero. An eyewitness later recalled that "every five minutes, at every intersection of the highway, women stopped him, the old women kissed him, telling him he was greater than Jesus Christ."[2]

For the people cheering Castro's progress, the young rebel leader had indeed become the national messiah. He had promised to restore democracy to the island, renouncing personal power and proclaiming the widely respected Judge Manuel Urrutia Lleó as the country's provisional president. His victory, however, meant much more to Cubans than political freedom. It promised to end decades of economic and political domination by the country's giant neighbor to the north, the United States, and to make the country truly independent for the first time in its history.

Despite his joyous welcome in Havana, however, Castro still faced an uncertain situation. Not all of the rebel groups that had opposed Batista recognized Castro's leadership. One such group, the Students' Revolutionary Directorate, had seized the University of Havana and had stolen weapons from the army headquarters, Camp Columbia.

CASTRO CHALLENGED the Directorate in a speech that night before 40,000 people gathered on Camp Columbia's parade ground. As he began to speak, someone released three white doves into the air. Two settled nearby, but one flew directly toward the podium and landed on Castro's shoulder. The onlookers saw this as a powerful omen. In Cuban mythology, the dove represents life. The incident added to the already powerful sense among those present that Castro enjoyed divine protection.[3]

With searchlights playing across the night sky above him, Castro spoke easily and forcefully, his powerful, high-pitched voice carrying through a hand-held microphone to the farthest reaches of the giant crowd. He challenged the Directorate to give up its stolen weapons and join in the formation of a new Cuba. "*Armas,¿ para qué?*," he asked. "Arms, for what? Why hide arms in different places in the capital? Why smuggle arms at this moment? For what? ... Arms, for what? To fight against whom? Against the revolutionary government that has the support of the whole people?" The eagerly listening crowd, caught up by the magic of his voice, roared back NO! Castro continued, "Arms, for what? To blackmail the president of the Republic? To threaten the government? To create organizations of gangsters? If we have a government of young and honorable men and if the country has faith in them, if we are going to have elections, why should arms be stored away?"[4]

The simple question *"Armas,¿ para qué?"* spread throughout the crowd and became a popular revolutionary slogan. The members of the Directorate, watching Castro's brilliant performance on television, were forced to admit that he had the support of the people. Later that night, they quietly surrendered their weapons to his men.

In the middle of his speech, Castro paused and turned to Camilo Cienfuegos, who was standing nearby. He asked, *"¿Voy bien, Camilo?"* ("Am I doing all right, Camilo?"). The gaunt, bearded rebel commander smiled and replied, *"Vas bien, Fidel"* ("You are doing all right"). The crowd shouted its approval, and another revolutionary slogan was born.[5]

Castro returned again and again to the theme of a new democracy for Cuba. "We cannot become dictators," he declared. "We shall never need to use force because we have the people, and because the people shall judge, and because the day the people want, I shall leave." He ended his speech by proclaiming, "I believe we have demonstrated sufficiently that we have fought without ambitions. I believe no Cuban has the slightest doubt about it." As he stepped from the podium, the crowd, which he had enthralled for two full hours, roared "FIDEL! FIDEL! FIDEL!"[6]

Many of the hopes and dreams that Havanans carried away from Camp Columbia that night were to go unfulfilled. Within two years, Castro abandoned his promises of democracy, taking over personal control of the government and turning Cuba into a Communist dictatorship allied with the Soviet Union. The repressive nature of his regime and the hardship caused by his construction of a Soviet-style, state-controlled economy prompted hundreds of thousands of Cubans to flee their country.

Yet in one important respect Castro fulfilled the expectations of his people. He stubbornly asserted Cuba's independence of the United States, breaking his country's historic ties to its northern neighbor. Castro and Cuba together braved the threat of American military attack and withstood harsh economic sanctions that crippled Cuba's economy. Castro's defiant independence left him the last of the world's great Communist revolutionaries in an age when most Communist regimes, including that of the Soviet Union, had crumbled into dust. He survived in large part because he fulfilled the national aspirations of his people, aspirations that are rooted deep in Cuba's past.

2

A Farmer's Son

When Christopher Columbus discovered Cuba and claimed it for Spain in 1492, he felt it to be "the most beautiful land that human eyes have ever seen."[1] Lofty mountains towered over fertile valleys, and flocks of colorful birds flew above dense forests of mahogany and cedar. The ocean abounded with fish and turtles, providing a rich supply of food for Cuba's native inhabitants, the Guanahatabeyes, Ciboneyes, and Tainos.

Columbus, who was searching for an ocean route to the Orient, mistook Cuba for part of the mainland of India. What he had found, however, was in fact the largest island in the Caribbean Sea. Lying less than 90 miles (150 kilometers) south of the Florida Keys, Cuba stretches for 745 miles (1,240 kilometers) from east to west. At its widest point it is no more than 100 miles (160 kilometers) across. Three great mountain ranges dominate Cuba's landscape: the Sierra de los Organos in the west, the Sierra de Trinidad in the center, and the majestic Sierra Maestra, the highest, in the east.

The first Spaniards who settled in Cuba were mainly interested in finding gold and silver. The settlers soon realized, however, that Cuba's fertile soil and mild climate made it an ideal place to grow sugarcane. Driven by a huge demand for sugar in Europe, planters burned down entire forests to make way for canefields and tried to enslave the natives to work them. The natives, unable to stand either the harsh labor or the new diseases brought by the Spanish to the island, quickly died out. The colonists replaced them with black slaves imported from Africa.

During the four centuries that Spain ruled Cuba, Spanish merchants earned huge profits from the sale of sugar grown by the Cuban-born descendants of the Spanish, known as Creoles. Sugar became a curse, however, for the Creoles themselves. With

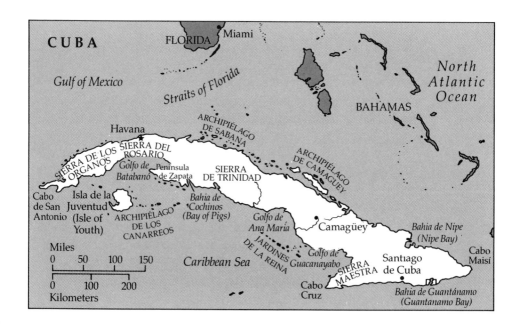

Field workers cut and gather sugarcane. Under Spanish rule, sugar became the mainstay of the Cuban economy.

every available acre of land planted with sugarcane, farmers could not grow food for themselves. The low prices paid for sugar by the merchants (who enjoyed a monopoly on the sugar trade) left many farmers with barely enough money to buy food for their families.

The contrast between the poverty in Cuba and the sugar wealth flowing to Spain, together with a growing desire on the part of upper-class Creoles for freer trade and greater influence in the island's government, eventually led Cubans to rebel against Spanish rule. Sporadic uprisings began in the early nineteenth century. In 1868 the first great war for Cuban independence, known as the Ten Years' War, broke out. Cuban rebels based in Oriente Province harassed the Spanish army with small, mobile groups of fighters, a technique known in Spanish as *la guerrilla*, "the little warfare."

Despite several early victories, the rebels were worn down by the superior numbers and better training of the Spanish forces. When a treaty was signed in 1878 that left Spain firmly in control of the island, many independence-minded Cubans fled to the United States.

One of these, a short, black-mustachioed poet named José Martí, organized a second revolution, which he launched with a landing in Oriente in April 1895. Although Martí himself was killed within weeks, the war he began lasted for three years, sweeping the length of Cuba and weakening Spain's grip on the island.

The war of 1895 brought the first direct involvement by the United States in the Cuban struggle for independence. Americans had long been interested in acquiring Cuba, both for its strategic position in the Caribbean Sea and for its wealth of natural resources. After the Ten Years' War, wealthy American investors had taken advantage of the devastation in Cuba to buy up sugar plantations and other businesses at bargain prices. As Martí's revolution swept the island, public opinion in the United States clamored for intervention to protect these business interests and to gain control of Cuba. In response, President William McKinley sent American warships to Cuban waters. On February 15, 1898, the battleship U.S.S. *Maine* blew up under mysterious circumstances in Havana harbor, with the loss of 266 lives. Americans eagerly went to war with Spain to the battle cry, "Remember the *Maine!*"

This 1898 print shows the destruction of the battleship *Maine* in Havana harbor.

The U.S. Army and Navy quickly forced the Spanish government to sue for peace. Only the desperate pleas of Cuban leaders, however, persuaded the United States to allow the formation of an independent Cuban republic. Cuban independence came at a price. In 1901, the U.S. government forced the Cubans to accept a special amendment to their constitution in exchange for self-rule. Named after its sponsor, Senator Orville Platt of Connecticut, the amendment prevented the Cuban government from making treaties with other countries and permitted the United States to intervene militarily in the island at will.

The Platt Amendment reduced Cuba to the status of an American dependency. When the Republic of Cuba was officially declared on May 20, 1902, the former American governor-general, Leonard Wood, wrote to President Theodore Roosevelt: "There is little or no real independence left to Cuba under the Platt Amendment."[2]

American occupation did much to benefit Cuba. The U.S. Army repaired war-damaged buildings, built roads and hospitals, improved health and sanitation, and established a system of public schools. However, American companies continued the process of buying up the island's economy. Firms such as Bethlehem Iron Works and Carnegie Steel Company gained control of Cuba's vast mineral resources, while other companies bought up its public utility networks. Most important, American investors interested in Cuba's sugar wealth bought land; by 1920 American companies would own two thirds of Cuba's farmland.

The strong American business presence and the threat of U.S. military intervention (the United States intervened in Cuba under the terms of the Platt Amendment three times between 1902 and 1917) cast a deep shadow over the young Cuban Republic. Men were elected president who aided American businesses in exchange for being made wealthy. As a result, graft and corruption in the Cuban government grew until using public office for private gain became a way of life.

It was during this troubled period in Cuba's history that a young man named Angel Castro emigrated to the island from Spain. Angel had served as a Spanish soldier in Cuba during the war of 1895–1898. In 1905, he returned to Cuba for good and settled in Oriente Province.

ANGEL FOUND HIMSELF in a land of stark contrasts. Oriente's landscape, with its rugged mountains overlooking broad expanses of green sugarcane fields, offered a vision of awe-inspiring beauty. Many of its inhabitants, however, lived in desperate poverty. Thousands of cane cutters and sugar mill workers, many black or mulatto, eked out their existence in shacks on the estates of wealthy Creole or American planters. During the four months of the cane harvest, when most people had work, workers earned less than one dollar a day. During the rest of the year unemployment soared as high as 50 percent, making starvation a very real danger.

Angel began his new life as a manual laborer. A hardworking, intelligent, and ambitious man, he soon set himself up as a contractor. He organized gangs of men to do jobs for hire, such as loading sugar into railroad cars for the American-based United Fruit Company, the largest sugar producer in the region.

Worker housing at a Cuban sugar plantation.

Angel was eventually able to start his own farm, which he called "Las Manacas," near the village of Birán, not far from the town of Mayari on the province's northern coast. He became an independent sugar producer, growing sugarcane and selling it to the United Fruit Company, whose lands surrounded his growing estate. Las Manacas ultimately became a plantation of some 26,000 acres (10,500 hectares) with 300 families living and working on the property.[3]

Sometime around 1910, Angel married a local schoolteacher named Maria Louisa Argota. They had two children, Pedro Emilio and Lidia. The marriage turned sour, however, after a pretty fourteen-year-old girl named Lina Ruz Gonzales joined the Castro household as a maid. Angel fell in love with Lina, who soon became pregnant. Maria Louisa promptly left her husband; the couple were eventually divorced.

The love-match between Angel and Lina produced a string of children. First came a girl, Angela, and then a boy, Ramón. On August 13, 1926, at 2:00 A.M., Lina gave birth to her third child, a strapping 10-pound (4.5-kilogram) boy whom the couple named Fidel Alejandro Castro Ruz. Lina eventually had four more children: Juana, Raúl, Emma, and Augustina.

Fidel developed into a big, active boy with a fierce temper and a stubborn streak. He grew up in wild surroundings. The Castros lived in a large wooden farmhouse, which was usually unkempt and overrun with chickens. Fidel spent most of his time playing outdoors, climbing hills, swimming in the nearby Birán River, and fishing or hunting.

Life on his father's estate exposed Fidel at an early age to the dominating American presence in Cuba. The wealthy lifestyle of the United Fruit Company's American employees stood in sharp contrast to the rampant poverty in the district. The contrast between the working conditions on United Fruit Company lands and those on the Castro estate was also marked. Although Angel Castro worked his men hard, he took care of their basic needs, something the United Fruit Company often failed to do for its workers. Fidel's elder brother Ramón later remembered: "My father was a very human man. Not one [of his workers] went to bed there without eating. . . . On the United Fruit Company lands, workers died of hunger."[4]

Fidel could not help but become aware of his own social superiority as the son of a wealthy planter. He recalled later in life: "Everyone lavished attention on me, flattered, and treated me differently from the other boys we played with when we were children. Those other children went barefoot while we wore shoes."[5] At age four, Fidel began to attend school in the nearby town of Marcane. He soon realized that he was also intellectually superior. He learned to read, for example, much more quickly than his classmates. The discovery of his talents gave Fidel an unshakable self-confidence.

The young boy reacted badly, however, to the authority of his teacher, Miss Felieu. He often got into violent arguments with her that ended in his running away, screaming curses. After one such incident, Fidel tripped and fell while running, landing on a board and piercing his tongue on a nail. When he got home his mother calmly remarked, "God punished you for swearing at the teacher." He later recalled, "I didn't have the slightest doubt that it was really true."[6]

Whether because of his rebelliousness or because of his talent, Miss Felieu convinced Fidel's parents that he, along with Ramón and Angela, should be sent away to Santiago de Cuba to school. When he was five years old, therefore, Fidel and his two siblings boarded a train to begin a new life in the provincial capital.

3

El Loco Fidel

For the young boy fresh from the canefields, the bustling city of Santiago was a new and overwhelming experience. Fidel was so excited by the huge train station with its high wooden arches, the crowds of people, and the noise that during his first night he wet his bed.[1]

The three Castro children went to live with Belén Felieu, the sister of their Birán schoolteacher, and her husband, Luis Hibbert, to receive private tutoring. The Hibberts, however, were more interested in taking the money Angel Castro paid them than in providing the children with a quality education. Fidel spent most of his time, lonely and miserably homesick, shut up in a room memorizing multiplication tables and practicing his handwriting.

After two years, Angel enrolled Fidel and Ramón in the La Salle Academy, a religious school in Santiago that catered to the sons of wealthy Oriente families. He continued, however, to board the boys with the Hibberts, a situation that Fidel found intolerable. One day, after Mr. Hibbert spanked him for misbehaving, Fidel's volatile temper boiled over, and he shouted insults and curses. He behaved so badly that Mr. Hibbert immediately sent him to live at the Academy as a boarder. Fidel later described the incident as "a great victory for me."[2]

Despite his father's wealth, Fidel did not fit in with the aristocratic children at the school. He was constantly teased for being the son of an immigrant peasant. Fidel responded to the taunts with his fists and his violent temper and quickly became known as a bully.

Nonetheless, Fidel enjoyed school. He was furious when his father, reacting to reports that he was fighting rather than studying, withdrew him from La Salle after his fourth-grade year and ordered him home. Fidel angrily threatened to burn the family house down unless his father allowed him to return.[3] After Lina, who valued schooling more than her self-educated husband, interceded, Angel relented and allowed Fidel to return to Santiago.

Angel and Lina decided, however, that Fidel might do better with stricter discipline. They transferred the stubborn nine-year-old to Santiago's Colegio Dolores, a school run by the Roman Catholic Society of Jesus, or the Jesuits. Surprisingly, Fidel flourished under the almost military discipline imposed by the Jesuit fathers. He studied harder and excelled in sports. Despite his continued love of fighting, he became popular with his fellow students.

Fidel's newfound popularity translated into influence. In 1940, one year before his graduation from Dolores, a local radio station held a poetry contest for the students, with the parents voting for the best entry. Although Fidel won, he later admitted that his poems "weren't the best, but I had made friends with all the boys. . . . Almost all the kids asked their parents to vote for me."[4]

With his improved performance at Dolores to back him up, Fidel persuaded his parents in the summer of 1941 to send him to the most prestigious high school in Cuba, the Jesuit-run Colegio de Belén (College of Bethlehem) in Havana. It was a daring step; Belén served the children of the nation's elite and had a national reputation for academic excellence.

In the fall, Fidel made the long train journey down the length of the island to Cuba's capital. The old colonial city, its Spanish elegance and sensuality mingled with the energy and vitality of American money, took his breath away. If he had hoped that his father's wealth would gain him quick acceptance among his fellow students at Belén, however, he was sadly disappointed. The sons of Havana's old moneyed families looked down with contempt on the big, gangling sixteen-year-old from the provinces, calling him *guajiro* ("peasant") behind his back.

Fidel channeled his anger into a burning desire to excel. He studied hard, doing particularly well in history, sociology, geography, and agriculture. His determination, concentration, and excellent memory gradually earned him respect. Fidel's powers of recall in particular were so amazing that, as one schoolmate later said, boys would gather and playfully ask him questions such as "Fidel, what does page forty-three of the sociology text say?" They would then listen in awe as Fidel recited the page in question, word for word.[5]

Fidel's academic success was mirrored by his success as an athlete. He dominated any sport he took up, from track and soccer to baseball and basketball. He often practiced on the basketball court until well after dark, earning himself the nickname *el loco Fidel*, "the crazy Fidel." Fidel became Belén's sports hero when he won the title of Cuba's best all-around school athlete for the school year 1943–1944.

Fidel's favorite subject at Belén was history. He developed a fascination for the lives of powerful, charismatic leaders such as the ancient Roman dictator Julius Caesar and Generalissimo Francisco Franco, the victor in the 1936–1939 Spanish Civil War.

Fidel found himself especially stirred, however, by the writings of José Martí, the tragic warrior-poet and organizer of the 1895 Cuban Revolution. Martí's passionate belief in social justice, poured out in a huge number of poems and essays written during his exile in Spain, Mexico, and the United States, touched a chord in Fidel, who had witnessed the hardship of Oriente's canefields. Martí wrote, "The nation where there are a few rich men is not rich: it [is] rich where everyone has a little of the wealth."[6]

Martí's writings also contained a vision of a united Latin America, which Martí regarded as "indispensable to the salvation and happiness of the peoples of America." Martí desired this union to protect Latin America not only from the Spanish but also from the growing power of the United States. He admired the freedom and idealism he saw in the great North American republic, but the expansionism that characterized the United States during the late nineteenth century frightened him. He tried to

The nineteenth-century revolutionary and poet José Martí became Castro's hero.

warn his countrymen about the danger posed in Cuba to Cuban independence by American influence. He wrote prophetically, "Once the United States is in Cuba, who will get it out?"[7]

Fidel's attachment to Martí bordered on worship. Similarities between Martí's life and his own, such as the fact that Martí was also the son of a Spanish soldier, made it easy for Fidel to identify with him. Throughout the rest of his life, Fidel constantly compared his actions to those of Martí, trying even to act, speak, and write like his hero. Martí's life became a yardstick by which Fidel measured his own success or failure.

The Jesuit fathers who ran Belén also exercised a powerful influence on Fidel. Unlike Catholic priests in other parts of Latin America, who were often born locally and took the side of the poor, the Jesuits at Belén came from Spain and were loyal to Cuba's aristocracy. They sought to influence Cuban society and politics by molding the children who would become Cuba's future leaders.

The Belén fathers immediately recognized Fidel as a boy with a great deal of leadership potential. They encouraged his growing thirst for knowledge and drilled into him their ideals of self-discipline and obedience to authority. They also encouraged his admiration of strong leaders, such as Franco, who put such ideals into practice in their governments.

The Jesuits gave Fidel a superb education. Their sense of discipline and order became a permanent part of his character. Fidel could not bring himself, however, to adopt their religion. During his childhood in Oriente, Fidel had absorbed a rural Christianity that emphasized compassion for the poor. He saw Belén's Jesuits as more committed to maintaining their own power in society than in teaching Christian ethics. He went through the daily religious rituals that they required, but he rejected them in his heart.

By the time Fidel graduated from Belén in 1945, his future looked bright with promise. He had talent and energy and the support of the Jesuits. His basketball coach, Father Francisco Barbeito, wrote in the Belén yearbook for 1945, "Fidel has what it takes and will make something of his life."[8] The eighteen-year-old farmer's son seemed poised to make the leap from his immigrant peasant roots to a place in the highest ranks of Cuban society.

Fidel decided to enter the University of Havana to study law. In the fall of 1945, he drove from Las Manacas to Havana in a brand-new Ford purchased for him by his father to begin his new life. Fidel's entry into the university was to be more, however, than the beginning of a brilliant career. It was to be his baptism into the tumultuous and violent world of Cuban politics.

4

The Young Radical

When nineteen-year-old Fidel Castro entered the University of Havana in the fall of 1945, the Republic of Cuba officially enjoyed a democratic government. The previous year Cubans had elected a university professor named Dr. Ramón Grau San Martín president of Cuba in an open and free vote. Grau headed the *Partido Revolucionario Cubano Auténtico* (Authentic Cuban Revolutionary Party). He replaced Fulgencio Batista, a former sergeant in the Cuban Army and political strongman who had ruled Cuba either as president or behind the scenes for the past decade.

Beneath the surface, however, Cuban political life was anything but democratic. President Grau employed bands of gangsters known as "action-groups" to support his government. He used the gangs against his political opponents, giving gang members government jobs in exchange for political killings. Grau's tactics led to open political warfare as progovernment action-groups battled with opposition gangs in the streets of Havana.

Much of this political violence erupted on the campus of the University of Havana. Set on a hill in the middle of the capital, the university had long served as a springboard to a political career. The university's student government in particular provided ambitious students with both a political training ground and a route into national politics; many members of the Cuban political elite had begun their careers in student government. Eager to control this gateway to power, the action-groups fought bitterly for command of the campus, terrorizing and occasionally murdering students and faculty members.

When Castro began his studies, two major gangs were competing for control of the campus. One was called the *Union Insurreccional Revolucionario* (Insurrectional Revolutionary Union) or UIR. The other, which had powerful connections with the Grau government, billed itself as the *Movimiento Socialista Revolucionario* (Socialist Revolutionary Movement) or MSR.

Castro found the highly charged political atmosphere at the university exhilarating. He plunged himself into student government, winning election as the representative of the law school's freshman class. His goal was to become president of the Federation of University Students (FEU), the student government's highest office.

The young law student quickly became popular. His tall, powerful physique; handsome, boyish face; and piercing brown eyes made a powerful impression. His physical courage in the face of gang-sponsored violence contributed to his popularity. He learned to carry a gun and threw himself into the gang melees that were a normal part of university life.

During Castro's freshman year, he went so far as to join a group planning the assassination of another student, a political rival named Lionel Gomez. The group waited for Gomez as he came out of the university stadium following a football match. When Gomez appeared, he was surrounded by several other people, which frightened his attackers. Castro was the only one to fire. He missed, however, hitting a fellow law student in the leg instead.

Both the UIR and the MSR pressed Castro to join them. Castro tried at first to gain the support of both gangs without joining either one. His desire to remain independent got him into trouble, though. He particularly angered the MSR by openly criticizing the Grau government. Toward the end of his freshman year, Mario Salabarria Aguilar, a prominent member of the MSR and one of the most powerful police chiefs in Havana, warned Castro to either stop his attacks on the government and choose between the UIR and the MSR or leave the university for good.

The ultimatum forced Castro into his first political crisis. He later recalled, "Alone, on the beach, facing the sea, I examined the situation. If I returned to the university, I would face personal danger, physical risk. . . . But not to return would be to give in to the threats, to admit my defeat by some killer, to abandon my own ideals and aspirations. I decided to return, and I returned—armed."[1] He began to associate himself with the UIR, although it is unclear whether he actually joined the action group.

Castro's independent nature kept him from advancing in the student government. Enrique Ovares, an architecture student and three-time FEU president, later remarked that "Fidel could never be elected president of the [law] school" because he would not work with others.² Even members of the campus Communist party, many of whom shared Castro's views on social justice, would not support him for student office because he could not be controlled. For his part, Castro came to admire the teachings of the Communist theorist Karl Marx, although he could not stomach the Communist party's rigid command structure and strict obedience to the central party in the Soviet Union.

Stymied in student politics, Castro looked outside the university for political opportunities. In early 1947, he began to associate himself with Eduardo "Eddy" Chibás, a plump, genial Auténticos politician who had become popular by criticizing President Grau.

In May 1947, Chibás formed an opposition party for disaffected Auténticos, which he called the *Partido del Pueblo Cubano* (Party of the Cuban People). The new party was nicknamed the *Ortodoxos* (the Orthodox) to indicate that it represented the true ideals of José Martí.

Although he admired Chibás, Castro had his doubts about the charismatic politician's plans to reform Cuba through the ballot box. As a child, Castro had seen his father paying bribes to local politicians to fix elections and had lost all respect for the electoral process. Castro felt that only armed revolution could rid Cuba of the evils that plagued it. He decided to form a small splinter party among younger members of the Ortodoxos. Called the *Acción Radical Ortodoxa* (Radical Orthodox Action), the group was committed to Chibás but advocated a revolutionary road to power.

IT WAS IN THE SUMMER OF 1947 that Castro first took part in a revolution. Political exiles from the Dominican Republic, on the nearby island of Hispaniola, had begun to assemble an invasion force in Cuba to depose the Dominican dictator, Rafael Trujillo. Castro eagerly joined the mixed group of Dominicans, Cubans, Venezuelans, and Costa Ricans in their bid to overthrow the brutal and corrupt Trujillo, who represented everything that he hated most.

The MSR controlled the Cuban contingent. This posed a problem for Castro, who still feared assassination by MSR hitmen. He was forced to arrange a temporary truce with the gang's leadership.

The small invasion force of 1,200 men waited on a tiny, mosquito-ridden island off the coast of Cuba for almost two months before hearing that the Grau administration had decided to stop the expedition. Castro's battalion sailed for Hispaniola anyway, only to be intercepted by the Cuban Navy.

With the expedition over, Castro's truce with the MSR was at an end. Yet he was surrounded by MSR fighters. As his ship sailed back to Cuba, he reportedly jumped overboard and swam several miles through shark-infested waters with his gun over his head before reaching shore.[3]

Once safely in Havana, Castro plunged back into national politics. With the election of 1948 growing near, he placed himself at the forefront of the campaign to elect Eddy Chibás president. In speeches that held his audiences spellbound, Castro blasted the Grau administration for its corruption and gang connections and attacked government officials and gang members by name.

Castro's outspokenness made him a renewed

A demonstrator carries a defaced portrait of Dominican dictator Rafael Trujillo. Castro took part in an unsuccessful attempt to overthrow Trujillo in 1947.

target for government agents and MSR thugs. The MSR made several attempts to kill him that failed only by sheer luck. In February 1948, however, when an assassin shot and killed an ex-leader of the MSR who had risen high in the Grau government, Castro was accused of leading the hit squad. The accusation, which was never substantiated, provided Castro's political enemies with a convenient excuse to hunt him down.

A sudden excuse to leave Cuba may have saved Castro's life. He was invited to attend a meeting in Bogotá, Colombia, scheduled for April 1948, to establish a Latin American student congress.

The Bogotá meeting unexpectedly provided Castro with the experience of a full-fledged revolution. On April 9, nine days after Castro's arrival in the city, a lone assassin killed Colombia's popular reformist leader, Jorge Eliécer Gaitán. The murder touched off an explosion of violence. Angry mobs attacked government buildings, smashed windows, tore down streetlights, and exchanged gunfire with government troops.

Castro could not resist the prospect of action. Using a rifle and ammunition obtained from a sympathetic policeman, he repeatedly risked his life trying to help the rioters overthrow the Colombian government. The uprising lasted for forty-eight chaotic hours and left more than three thousand people dead. Castro survived unharmed and was flown out of the country with other Cuban students by the Cuban embassy.

The Bogotá riots had a profound impact on Castro. He was impressed by the violent power generated by the angry mobs. Yet he had noticed that the rioters had lacked organized leadership. He was convinced that had such a revolutionary leadership existed, the popular forces in Bogotá would have seized power in a matter of hours.

On his return to Cuba, Castro rejoined Chibás's presidential campaign. He learned a great deal from watching the Ortodoxos leader in action. Chibás exploited his personal charm to win over his audiences. He also made powerful use of symbols, such as a broomstick to represent the sweeping away of evil, and slogans, such as *vergüenza contra dinero* ("dignity against money"), to capture the popular imagination.4 Perhaps most important, Chibás exploited the mass appeal of radio. His Sunday afternoon broadcasts, in which he blasted the Grau administration for its violence and corruption, commanded such attention that they regularly brought the country to a standstill.

THE CAMPAIGN TRAIL left Castro little time for socializing. Preoccupied with politics and painfully shy around women, he often canceled what few dates he made to attend political meetings. Castro's behavior changed, however, when he met a pretty, green-eyed philosophy student from a wealthy Oriente family named Mirta Díaz-Balart. Castro fell in love and somehow found time for a successful courtship. On October 12 the couple were married in Mirta's hometown of Banes, in a lavish ceremony paid for by the delighted Angel Castro.

The wedding was overshadowed by the electoral defeat of Eddy Chibás. An Auténtico politician named Carlos Prío Socarrás succeeded Grau to the presidency.

Eduardo Chibás, the flamboyant leader of the Ortodoxos, brandishes a gun in an emotional confrontation with police. He was protesting the use of tear gas against demonstrators.

Castro placed himself once more in the forefront of the opposition. His angry attacks on Prío forced him to go into hiding in the United States for a few months to avoid gang reprisals. The only bright spot in Castro's troubled life came on September 14, 1949, when his son was born. Following Cuban tradition, the couple named the boy after his father, christening him Fidel Castro Díaz-Balart, or Fidelito for short.

In 1950, Castro decided that it was finally time for him to graduate from the university. His political activities, however, had left him far behind his classmates. Taking advantage of his tremendous discipline and memory, Castro studied night and day throughout the spring and summer of 1950 and completed two years worth of work in six months. In September he graduated with a Doctor of Law degree.

The years that Castro spent at the University of Havana provided his first and most important training for what lay ahead. He had honed his skills as a politician and orator and had seen electoral campaigning and revolutionary violence firsthand. More important, he had learned to stay alive by watching his back and trusting no one but himself. Later in life he would remark that the five years he spent at the university had been more dangerous than the entire time he spent as a guerrilla in the Sierra Maestra.[5]

5

"History Will Absolve Me!"

After his graduation, Castro set up a small law office with two classmates, Jorge Aspiazo and Rafael Resende, in an old, run-down section of Havana. The trio took cases from poor workers, street vendors, and students. They often accepted goods such as food or furniture rather than money in payment. As a result, the firm of Aspiazo, Castro, and Resende barely earned enough money to pay its office rent.

Without a steady income, Castro and Mirta lived with their small son on the brink of poverty. Castro largely ignored his family's situation. His first love remained politics. Eddy Chibás had launched a second campaign for the presidency. With the elections of 1952 drawing near, Castro threw himself into the effort to bring victory to the Ortodoxos cause.

Disaster struck, however, on Sunday, August 5, 1951, when Chibás, devastated by Auténticos charges that he had fabricated evidence of government corruption, shot himself during his regular weekly radio broadcast. Castro, who was at the station, rushed Chibás to the hospital. He watched at his mentor's bedside for eleven days until Chibás died on August 16.

Chibás's suicide created a backlash of sympathy for the Ortodoxos that made the party's victory in the upcoming elections almost certain. Despite his distrust of the electoral process, Castro decided to take advantage of the situation and run for a seat in the Cuban Congress.

The young lawyer launched a dynamic campaign. His skillful and impassioned oratory attacking government corruption, President Prío, and even the top members of his own party became extremely popular with his working-class audiences. By early 1952, there seemed little doubt in his or anyone else's mind that he would win a seat in Congress. The Ortodoxos, too, seemed poised for victory. Public opinion polls indicated that the man who had replaced Chibás as the head of the party, Roberto Agramonte, would easily defeat his lackluster Auténticos opponent, Carlos Hevia.

Only one other candidate contested the presidential race. Fulgencio Batista, who had lived for the last six years in luxury in Florida, returned to Cuba to run for a second presidential term. The polls indicated, however, that he had little chance of victory.

All of that changed on the morning of March 10, 1952. At 2:40 A.M., Batista strolled into the army headquarters at Camp Columbia, where officers loyal to him had already seized control. Batista got on the telephone and quickly received assurances of support from the military commanders of the other Cuban provinces. Within a few hours, he had taken control of the entire country.

Batista is surrounded by supporters at Cuban army headquarters as he takes control of the country on March 10, 1952.

When news of the coup reached Castro, he was at home asleep. Fearing arrest, he immediately fled to the nearby apartment of his older sister, leaving Mirta and Fidelito behind. His fear of Batista's police was well founded. A few hours after he left, policemen came to his apartment in search of him.

Cuba's university students responded angrily to the coup, staging mass protest meetings across the country. The Ortodoxos leadership wavered, however, before finally issuing a tame call for nonviolent resistance to the new dictatorship. Castro was furious. Six days after the coup, when the top Ortodoxos met at the tomb of Eddy Chibás to pay tribute to their fallen leader, Castro appeared— uninvited. He climbed up on a nearby tombstone and shouted angrily that only force, not nonviolence, could overthrow Batista.[1]

THROUGH HIS CONNECTIONS in the Ortodoxos youth movement, Castro quickly began building a network of people who shared his belief in armed revolution. The most important of these were Abel Santamaría, a slender, sandy-haired accountant for the Pontiac Corporation in Havana, and his sister Haydee. Their tiny two-room apartment, in a building at the corner of O and 25th streets in Havana, became the center of Castro's budding revolutionary movement.[2]

The months following the coup were difficult ones for Mirta. With Castro in hiding and devoting all of his energies to his revolution, she and Fidel lived apart most of the time. One evening Castro came home to find that the power company had cut off the electricity to their apartment. Mirta sat in total darkness with the three-year-old Fidelito, who was ill with a high fever. Castro borrowed five pesos from a friend to give to his wife, although he had a hundred pesos in his pocket. He had collected the money to buy guns, and he refused to use it for anything else.[3]

Castro's callous behavior toward Mirta was compounded by his infidelity. In November 1952, Castro met Natalia "Naty" Revuelta, a doctor's wife who had helped to raise money for his movement, and fell in love with her. Naty succumbed to the charms of the young revolutionary, and the two began a long love affair.

As 1953 opened, Castro and Santamaría began to plan their uprising. They decided to attack the Moncada Barracks, an army base in Santiago, in the hopes of sparking a general revolt in Oriente Province. A simultaneous attack on an army post at Bayamo, 60 miles (100 kilometers) to the northwest, would prevent the government from sending reinforcements to Santiago.

Castro had by now built up an organization of some 1,200 men grouped into about 150 cells throughout Havana and the nearby province of Pinar del Río. He handpicked 150 men and ordered them to begin traveling to Santiago in the third week of July 1953. He shipped the weapons he had laboriously collected to a rented farm just outside the city.

During the night of July 25–26, the rebels gathered in the farmhouse. None of them knew as yet why they had been summoned. At 3:00 A.M. Castro arrived. He called the group together (which included, in addition to the men, Haydee Santamaría and another woman, Melba Hernández), and told them that he intended to attack the Moncada Barracks at dawn. A gasp at the boldness of the plan traveled around the room. Castro then offered anyone who wished a chance to back out. Only ten men decided to leave.

At 5:00 A.M. on July 26, twenty-six cars left the farmhouse for Santiago. The rebels were dressed in homemade and ill-fitting military uniforms to confuse Moncada's defenders. They had an assortment of weapons that included U.S. Army rifles, hunting rifles, revolvers, and one ancient machine gun with which to defeat roughly one thousand well-trained and well-armed soldiers.

The attack began as planned. Shortly after 5:15 A.M., the main attack force under Castro took one of the gates to the barracks and arrested the guards. A detachment that included Castro's brother Raúl seized the roof of the nearby Palace of Justice to provide covering fire, while Abel Santamaría captured a hospital building whose windows also overlooked the barracks.

Nothing else went right. An army patrol surprised Castro's group before it could enter the compound. A confused firefight broke out, and the barracks' garrison was given time to respond. After a battle that lasted about an hour, Castro ordered a retreat. He left behind three dead and several wounded. His men had killed nineteen soldiers.

The attack at Bayamo also failed. The fleeing rebels scattered in all directions. Castro himself took a small group and headed on foot for the Sierra Maestra in hopes of continuing the struggle.

The army reacted savagely to the Moncada attack. Soldiers and members of the Oriente Rural

Guard hunted down and captured many of the rebels. They put most of those they caught to death,
often after torturing them first. One of those who
died in this fashion was Abel Santamaría.

The country reacted with shock and outrage to
the army's brutality. Public opinion swung strongly
over to the side of the rebels, who were now known
as the *Moncadistas.*

On the morning of August 1, a Rural Guard
patrol surprised and captured Castro and two others
in a shack in the mountains. Only the fact that the
lieutenant in charge of the patrol had known Castro
at the university saved the rebel leader's life. The
lieutenant had the wit to deliver his captive, in full
view of the public, to Santiago's civilian jail rather
than to the military prison, a move that prevented
the army from killing Castro in secret.

The trial of the Moncadistas began on September 21, 1953, in Santiago's Palace of Justice. Twenty-
six survivors of the attack stood trial, together with
Haydee Santamaría and Melba Hernández. Castro
appeared in court in his favorite dark blue striped
suit, his hair carefully combed, and his new pencil-
mustache neatly trimmed.4

The court gave Castro permission to act as his
own defense attorney. Castro used his legal training
to devastating effect, forcing witnesses for the government to admit to the torture and murder of his
men and visibly moving the sympathy of the large
audience over to his side. The government moved
quickly to silence him. His jailers kept him from
attending the court's third session on September 26,
claiming that he was ill. They continued to keep him
imprisoned even after a visit from the court's three
judges determined him to be perfectly healthy.

Although he suppressed opposition, Batista later sought to give his dictatorship the appearance of democracy. This towering billboard was set up for a 1954 election campaign.

ESTE ES EL HOMBRE

Sin Odio ni Rencor

CORTESIA DE CARLOS FERNANDEZ CAMPOS

On October 16, after his compatriots had already been found guilty and sentenced, Castro was again brought to trial. This time, the proceedings were held in the tiny nurses' lounge of the hospital in an effort to keep out the public.

In a two-hour speech in his own defense, Castro linked the Moncada uprising to the long Cuban tradition of revolution. "I bring in my heart the doctrines of Martí and in my mind the noble ideas of all men who have defended the freedom of the people," he declared. "We have incited a rebellion against a single illegitimate power which has usurped and concentrated in its hands the legislative and executive powers of the nation."

Castro ended his speech with a reminder of the brutality that he and his men had endured. "As for me, I know that jail will be as hard as it has ever been for anyone," he admitted, "filled with threats, with vileness, and cowardly brutality; but I do not fear this, as I do not fear the fury of the miserable tyrant who snuffed out the lives of seventy of my brothers." His final words rang through the tiny room: "*¡Condenádme, no importa! ¡La historia me absolverá!*" ("Condemn me, it does not matter! History will absolve me!")[5]

The room remained silent after Castro finished. Finally, one of the judges hurriedly condemned him to fifteen years in prison.

A waiting crowd cheered Castro as he was escorted from the hospital. Although the Moncada uprising had failed miserably, Castro had achieved what he had striven for ever since he had launched his political career. The trial had discredited the government and had catapulted him to national fame.

6

Víctory

On October 17, 1953, Castro walked into Building 1 of the Presidio Modelo prison hospital and greeted his surprised and elated companions. His fellow Moncadistas had been in the Presidio, a prison on the Isle of Pines some 60 miles (100 kilometers) off the southwest coast of Cuba, since October 13. They had spent four gloomy days worrying that Castro had been executed or that he was being kept separate from them.

Castro quickly gave his men a new sense of hope. He told them that they were not there simply to serve their sentences but to prepare for a new revolution. He set up a school with the grandiose title of the Abel Santamaría Ideological Academy. Each morning, the Moncadistas studied history, mathematics, literature, geography, and political theory, with Castro doing most of the teaching.[1]

To keep himself before the public eye, Castro laboriously smuggled the text of his "History Will Absolve Me" speech out of prison. Throughout the first part of 1954, he sent the text piece by piece to Melba Hernández and Haydee Santamaría, who were released from prison in February. The two women printed thousands of copies, which sympathizers distributed all over Cuba.

In July, Castro was stunned to receive the news that his wife Mirta had briefly held a position in Batista's Ministry of the Interior. He also learned that she was planning to divorce him. Castro was apparently unconcerned by the fact that Mirta had no means of support while he was in prison. Nor did he display any understanding of the isolated life his revolutionary activities had condemned her to lead. He was outraged that she had accepted money from his sworn enemies, discrediting him as an opposition leader.

Despite his embarrassment and anger, Castro refused to give up his resistance to the Batista regime. When an official visited him and offered him amnesty if he would stop his attacks on the government, Castro responded defiantly, "One thousand years of prison before I renounce any of my principles."[2]

Amnesty for Castro and his men, however, fitted Batista's political needs. Searching for ways to improve his image with the Cuban people, the dictator decided to release all political prisoners in Cuban jails. On May 7, 1955, the Moncadistas suddenly found themselves free men.

Batista had underestimated Castro's determination. Once out of prison, the rebel leader promptly began a new and spirited campaign against the government. Castro blasted Batista on the radio, in public speeches, and in the newspapers. His outspokenness quickly provoked a government crackdown on the opposition. Fearing renewed imprisonment or even death if he remained in Cuba, Castro decided to flee the country.

ON JULY 7, 1955, only six weeks after his release from prison, Castro left Cuba for Mexico City. Within days of his arrival, he began laying the groundwork for a new revolution. Operating from quarters in a run-down hotel, he made the rounds of the city, seeking out Cuban exiles and wealthy Mexicans sympathetic to his cause. Through Melba Hernández, he remained in close touch with his supporters in Cuba, who were now calling themselves the 26th of July Movement, or M-26-7, in memory of the Moncada attack.

One of the first people Castro met in Mexico turned out to be one of the most important. A mutual friend introduced him to an intense, asthmatic doctor from Argentina named Ernesto "Che" Guevara. Che was a committed Communist. Only two years younger than Castro, he had traveled extensively in Central and South America and had seen firsthand the terrible poverty that gripped much of the continent. He burned with desire to free the poor of Latin America from what he saw as their oppression by the wealthy, and harbored a fierce hatred of the United States.

Che and Castro stayed up the entire night of their first meeting discussing politics and revolution. By the next morning, Che had joined Castro's movement. He later recalled, "It did not take much to incite me to join any revolution against tyranny, but Fidel impressed me as an extraordinary man."[3]

Castro hoped to launch his revolution with a Martí-like invasion of his homeland. He drew up plans to land in western Oriente with a small force of eighty men, which would be met by M-26-7 members who had remained in Cuba. The invasion would coincide with a call for a nationwide general strike and with uprisings in Santiago and other cities. If the invasion failed, the rebels would retreat to the Sierra Maestra to begin a guerrilla war.

Castro aimed at invading Cuba before the end of 1956. The longer he remained in exile, the greater the risk that others would take over leadership of the revolutionary opposition there. In late June 1956, however, he was arrested by the Mexican government, which was under pressure from Batista to put a stop to his activities. Castro was only able to win his release with the help of a sympathetic Mexican lawyer.

Once out of jail, Castro redoubled his efforts to launch his invasion before the end of the year. He brushed aside objections from the M-26-7 leader in Santiago, Frank País, that the M-26-7 cells in Cuba were as yet too poorly organized and underfunded to launch a successful uprising.

Castro purchased and refurbished an old 38-foot (11.5-meter) motor yacht called the *Granma*. On the night of November 24, 1956, he gathered his men (the *Fidelistas*) in pouring rain at the little Mexican port of Tuxpan, where the *Granma* was berthed. Despite storm warnings, he refused to delay. His men boarded the tiny boat, crowding together so that only half of them could sit at one time. At 12:20 A.M. Castro climbed aboard. The *Granma* cast off and slowly chugged away into the rainy blackness.

Mexican authorities arrested twenty-two Cuban exiles for plotting against Batista. Among them were Castro, indicated by the arrow, and Che Guevara, seated second from the left.

The Fidelistas battled seasickness and fear as waves pounded their tiny craft. They had to bail frantically just to keep the *Granma* afloat. Although the weather cleared by the third day, the storm put the expedition far behind schedule. Castro had hoped to land in Cuba on November 30. When that day arrived, however, the *Granma* still had 180 miles (300 kilometers) to go.

The battered rebels could only listen with horror and frustration to radio reports of the M-26-7 uprising in Santiago, which Frank País loyally staged on schedule. Without Castro's invasion force to support it, the uprising failed after thirty hours of bitter fighting. Other M-26-7 actions on the island also collapsed. When Castro landed, he would be staging his revolution alone.

At 5:00 A.M. on December 2, the *Granma* finally reached Cuba. The yacht went aground more than a mile away from where the M-26-7 reception party waited. In the resulting shipwreck, the expedition lost all of its food and heavy weapons.

No sooner had the Fidelistas dragged themselves out of the surf than they were spotted by a Cuban Navy patrol boat. The rebels quickly came under fire from ships and aircraft and were forced to flee inland. After wading through a mangrove swamp, the exhausted men finally reached dry land. Undaunted by the disaster, Castro strode up to the first peasant they saw and declared, "I am Fidel Castro and we have come to liberate Cuba."[4]

Four days later, another peasant betrayed the Fidelistas to government forces. In the ambush that followed, the army destroyed Castro's expedition, killing or capturing all but sixteen of his men. Castro and his brother Raúl escaped, as did Che, who received a wound in his neck.

The Cuban government announced that its forces had wiped out Castro's entire army and that Castro himself had been killed. Castro, however, refused to cooperate. After bringing his handful of men to the safety of the Sierra Maestra, he gathered them together and staged a successful attack on a small army outpost in the town of La Plata, not far from Bayamo. The victory netted the rebels weapons, food, and medical supplies and provided them with a badly needed morale boost.

Castro knew, however, that he needed more than one small victory to keep his struggle alive. He had to let the Cuban people know that he was still alive and fighting.

At the end of January 1957, he sent word to his supporters in Havana that he wanted to meet with a foreign journalist, preferably an American. Castro's offer reached *The New York Times*, which promptly sent one of its senior editors, Herbert L. Matthews, to the Sierra Maestra.

The balding, fifty-seven-year-old Matthews met Castro, who by now was sporting a scraggly black beard, at a mountain rendezvous on the morning of February 17. Castro set out to create the impression that his handful of rebels represented a major combat force. While he and Matthews discussed Cuba's future, his men marched past repeatedly, each time wearing different clothes. Castro himself occasionally referred to other, nonexistent, guerrilla camps in the area to make it seem as though he had a large army at his disposal.

Eager for a big scoop, Matthews took the bait. In his article, which appeared on February 24, he painted the Fidelistas in glowing terms and described them as a major threat to the Batista regime. The story gave M-26-7 sudden international prestige and made Castro a romantic hero in the United States.

The article had a huge impact in Cuba itself. Proof of Castro's survival gave him an aura of invincibility and made him appear as Cuba's man of destiny. His apparent command of a major army raised

In the Sierra Maestra, Castro and his followers pose for news photographers. News coverage helped make him a romantic hero in the United States.

M-26-7 to a position of sudden leadership among the Cuban opposition. As a result, money began to flow from all across the island into Castro's empty coffers.

BY THE SPRING OF 1957, the skeleton of a real army had begun to take shape in the mountains. Mountain peasants and idealistic young men from the cities swelled the Fidelistas' ranks. As the rebels won victory after victory in clashes with government troops, they expanded their sphere of influence until it embraced the entire Sierra Maestra.

As the war intensified, Castro found himself increasingly relying on a young woman named Celia Sánchez for assistance. Celia had originally served as the Fidelistas' connection with the outside world, collecting supplies for them and making sure the shipments got past government patrols. After meeting Castro personally for the first time in February 1957, she moved into the mountains and rapidly became his most trusted aide and companion.

Calm and organized where Castro was flamboyant and impulsive, Celia turned his grand schemes into functioning reality. She made Castro rest when he was exhausted and kept him from personally leading his men into battle. The two rapidly became dependent on each other; many later suspected that the relationship became romantic. Although Celia and Castro never married, Celia would remain at Castro's side for the rest of her life.

At the same time that he was fighting Batista's soldiers, Castro had to contend with a growing split within M-26-7 itself. Leaders of the lowland M-26-7 cells, led by Frank País in Santiago, opposed Castro's dictatorial control of the organization. They felt that a nationwide general strike, not the mountain war, would ultimately overthrow Batista. They were also disturbed by what they saw as Castro's lack of a concrete political program.

On July 12, 1957, Castro tried to heal the breach by releasing the Sierra Maestra Manifesto, a document jointly signed by him, Raúl Chibás, brother of Eddy and the leader of the Ortodoxos, and Felipe Pazos, an economist with ties to former President

Prío. The Manifesto called for democracy, a free press, and land reform.

The following February, in an interview published in the American magazine *Coronet*, Castro expanded on his vision of the future. He proclaimed that he was "fighting to do away with dictatorship in Cuba and establish the foundations of genuine representative government." He renounced any personal role as Cuba's leader and called for freedom for all political prisoners, an end to corruption, and a new campaign to teach every Cuban to read and write. In a remark clearly aimed at the United States, he denied having any plans to take over foreign property.[5]

Castro allowed the lowland M-26-7 leadership to persuade him to call a national strike for April 9, 1958. Although thousands of Cuban workers answered the call and put down their tools, the strike failed to oust Batista, primarily because of a lack of coordination between M-26-7 and other Cuban opposition groups. The fiasco discredited the lowlanders and left Castro firmly in charge of his movement.

The failure of M-26-7's urban cadres prompted Castro to make overtures to the Cuban Communist party, which was called the *Partido Socialista Popular* (Popular Socialist Party) or PSP. He hoped to gain access to the PSP's highly disciplined organization among Cuba's urban workers. Castro realized, however, that bitter anti-Communist feelings in the United States made the U.S. government deeply suspicious of any Cuban revolutionary group with Communist ties. He therefore hid his Communist connections, welcoming PSP emissaries to his mountain headquarters but publicly denying any links to their party.

In the summer of 1958, Batista launched his final offensive against the Fidelistas. In a desperate attempt to end a war that was slowly but surely weakening his powerful grip, the dictator threw 10,000 troops and the cream of his air force against a rebel army that still numbered only in the hundreds.

Much of Batista's air force had been supplied by the United States. Batista ordered his planes to bomb the Sierra Maestra despite attempts by the United States to discourage him from using U.S.-built weapons against his own people. The air raids had little effect on Castro's guerrillas but hit the local peasant population hard. The sight of American weapons killing Cuban peasants inflamed the feelings of resentment toward the United States that Castro had harbored since childhood. In a letter to Celia, Castro wrote of witnessing one attack:

> *When I saw the rockets firing . . . at Mario's house, I swore to myself that the Americans were going to pay dearly for what they are doing. When this war is over, a much wider and bigger war will commence for me: the war that I am going to wage against them. I am aware this is my true destiny.*[6]

Batista's offensive fell apart after seventy-six days. A triumphant Castro responded with an offensive of his own. The bearded Fidelistas, stunned after two years of hard fighting to find that they were actually winning, swept down the length of the island capturing village after village. On New Year's Day, 1959, they heard the news that Batista had fled the country. The next day, Castro entered Santiago, the first step on the road that would lead him at last to Havana.

7

Braving the Eagle's Wrath

During the first few weeks after his victory, Castro maintained that he was only interested in serving as the commander in chief of Cuba's armed forces. He allowed Provisional President Urrutia to organize a government made up mainly of moderate opposition leaders and to name José Miro Cardona, the former president of the Cuban Bar Association, as his prime minister. After forming his government, Urrutia proceeded to dissolve the Cuban Congress, fire all provincial governors, mayors, and town councilmen, and remove Batista supporters from their posts in the government bureaucracy.

Castro, who could not bring himself to stay out of the limelight, spent most of his time driving through Havana. He harangued the large crowds that gathered around him with impromptu speeches condemning the evils of Batista's regime and promising dramatic change. He often announced—without consulting Urrutia—the government's intention of undertaking major reform programs.

These impromptu remarks caused enormous frustration for the president and his advisers.

Havanans responded to Castro with an affection that bordered on worship. A Presbyterian minister, carried away by the current of pro-Castro feeling sweeping the city, declared, "Fidel Castro is an instrument in the hand of God for the establishment of his reign among men."[1]

Castro also displayed the darker side of his nature in the early days of his revolution. In response to public pressure, he authorized his brother Raúl to begin the summary trials and executions of Batista operatives believed to be guilty of political killings and other acts of brutality. Seventy men were quickly tried and executed, including three former Batista commanders who were given a public "show trial" in Havana's sports stadium.

Hundreds of people were tried and executed over the following months. Not all were equally guilty. In March, a revolutionary tribunal in Santiago acquitted forty-four pilots, bombardiers, and mechanics from Batista's air force on charges of bombing peasants in the Sierra Maestra. Outraged, Castro demanded a new trial, declaring on television that "revolutionary justice is not based on legal precepts, but on moral conviction." The airmen were retried and sentenced to prison terms.

It soon became clear that Castro, not Urrutia, ruled Cuba in the minds of the Cuban people. In mid-February, Prime Minister Miro Cardona resigned in protest. Miro Cardona persuaded Urrutia to make Cuba's government match reality by naming Castro himself as the country's new prime minister.

Castro's appointment as prime minister brought mixed reactions in the United States. While a wide

Castro reads the oath of office on being sworn in as prime minister on February 16. Beside him (left) is President Urrutia.

section of the American population still regarded Castro as an idealistic reformer, others, particularly those with business interests in Cuba, believed that he had links to the Communists and feared that he might decide to nationalize American property. Castro's critics also pointed to the continuing executions as an indication that the young revolutionary was not as pure as he seemed.

Toward the end of February 1959, the American Society of Newspaper Editors invited Castro to visit the United States. He accepted and left Cuba on April 15. The trip was a huge success. As Castro traveled from Boston to New York and Washington, D.C., large and enthusiastic crowds greeted him at every stop. When he spoke at the National Press Club in Washington, he drew the largest turnout in the club's history.[2]

Castro tried to persuade the American people that his revolution was not a threat to their interests. He repeated over and over that he was not a Communist and that the Communists had no influence over him. In an appearance before the Senate Foreign Relations Committee, he promised that Cuba would stand with the United States against its enemy the Soviet Union and that he would protect all foreign businesses in Cuba.

CASTRO'S EXPRESSIONS OF GOODWILL toward the United States concealed an entirely different agenda. Castro did not intend to create a Cuban democracy in which the United States would continue to call the tune. He planned instead to free Cuba's government and economy from American control and to end the poverty and illiteracy that plagued most of the island's population.

Castro sensed accurately that most Cubans valued housing, education, health care, and an end to government corruption far more than they valued elections. Accordingly, during the first months after his victory he ordered rents cut in half for the poorest city dwellers and launched a massive building program in the countryside. New homes, hospitals, and schools sprang up across the island, connected by hundreds of miles of new rural roads.

To put a stop to political corruption, Castro made stealing from the government punishable by death. He also outlawed prostitution and gambling, two prominent features of Cuban society under Batista.

The capstone of Castro's reform program was his campaign for adult literacy. Hundreds of young Cubans, known as "alphabetizers," flooded the countryside in a massive effort to teach the island's adult population to read.

Castro's plans to redistribute Cuba's land posed the most direct threat to American interests. On May 17, 1959, Castro signed a new Agrarian Reform Law. The law limited land ownership to 1,000 acres (405 hectares), except for important sugar and rice plantations. All land over the legal limit was to be seized by the government and given to the farmers who worked it or to farmers' collectives.

To administer the new law, Castro set up the National Institute for Agrarian Reform (INRA). His new creation quickly became more than an agency for land redistribution. INRA took over control of everything from health care to housing, education, and road building, becoming in effect a second government through which Castro could push forward his reforms.

Castro explains his land reform program to farmers at a small village in eastern Cuba.

To speed up the reform process, Castro turned once more to the Communists for help. The PSP's superb national organization was an ideal tool for extending reform to every corner of the island. The Communists also offered Castro another important advantage. Alliance with the PSP made it more likely that the Soviet Union would support Castro if the United States tried to overthrow him.

Castro quietly moved Communist politicians into important government positions even as he continued to deny publicly that he had any Communist ties. The growing importance of the PSP caused serious discontent within both the government and the ranks of Castro's own followers.

Castro responded ruthlessly. In July 1959, he forced President Urrutia, who had tried to spearhead the anti-Communist opposition, to resign. Three months later, he ordered his friend and loyal follower Hubert Matos, the military commander of Camagüey Province, and thirty-eight of his officers put on trial for treason after Matos protested the appointment of Castro's pro-Communist brother Raúl as minister of the armed forces. Although no charges of treason were ever proved, Matos was sentenced to twenty years in prison.

Castro's drift toward communism sparked severe opposition among Cuba's educated classes. Many middle- and upper-class Cubans who had supported M-26-7 wanted only a return to democracy, not a radical overhaul of Cuban society in favor of the poor. Some, appalled by Castro's betrayal of his democratic promises, began to join opposition groups. Others, mainly doctors, technicians, and other professionals with skills vital to Cuba's economy, fled to the United States. There they joined a growing community of Cuban exiles that was committed to Castro's overthrow.

Castro responded to the opposition with an appeal to the people. At a convention of sugar workers in December 1959, he called for ordinary men and women to come to the defense of the Revolution. "We shall have to defend the revolution with arms in 1960," he declared. "We shall fight to the last man."[3] Castro asked his listeners to denounce enemies of the Revolution to the police. By the end of the year, large numbers of Castro's political opponents had been arrested, with little assurance of a fair trial.

In January 1960, the government demanded that Cuban newspapers printing stories critical of the Revolution include "clarifications" giving the official government position. The move clearly signaled the end of a free press in Cuba and caused great anger among Cuban journalists. Several newspapers refused to comply with the order. They were summarily closed.

The visit to Cuba in February 1960 of Soviet Vice-Premier Anastas Mikoyan bolstered Castro's hopes for Soviet aid. Mikoyan praised Castro's land reform program and signed a major trade agreement with Cuba. In the agreement, the Soviet Union promised to buy sugar and other Cuban products and to supply the island with oil, steel, iron, and other essentials, as well as with technicians to replace those who had fled.

THE PRESIDENT OF THE UNITED STATES, Dwight D. Eisenhower, was alarmed by Castro's expanding relationship with the Soviets. Ever since the end of

World War II in 1945, the United States had been locked in an intense political, economic, and ideological competition with the Soviet Union, popularly called the Cold War, over the issue of Soviet attempts to spread communism. Eisenhower felt that Castro's overtures to the Soviet Union posed an intolerable threat to American national security by offering the Soviets a chance to expand their influence into the Western Hemisphere.

On March 17, 1960, Eisenhower authorized the U.S. Central Intelligence Agency (CIA) to arm and train a force of Cuban exiles for an invasion of their homeland. Without Eisenhower's knowledge, the CIA went one step further and tried to eliminate Castro himself. The agency's plans ranged from the violent to the ridiculous. CIA operatives tried to hire Mafia hit men to kill the Cuban leader. Other plans included poisoning Castro's cigars and destroying his charismatic appeal by dusting his shoes with a chemical that would make his beard fall out. None of these schemes made it past the planning stage.[4]

On May 7, 1960, Castro established formal diplomatic relations with the Soviet Union. On May 23, his government notified foreign oil companies with refineries in Cuba, which included Texaco, Standard, and Royal Dutch, that they would have to begin refining oil imported from Russia. When they refused, Castro ordered their Cuban property seized.

The Eisenhower administration responded on July 6 by drastically cutting American imports of Cuban sugar. The move was a sharp blow to the Cuban sugar industry, which depended heavily on the United States for its sales. Castro fired back by ordering all American businesses in Cuba to submit their inventories and operating records to his government for inspection, a first step toward their nationalization. His hand was strengthened by the Soviet Union, which promised to make up the loss from the cut in U.S. sugar imports.

In this atmosphere of extreme tension, Castro made his second visit to the United States as Cuba's leader. On September 18, 1960, he left Cuba to attend a meeting of the United Nations General Assembly in New York City. Castro could not resist fanning the flames of American hostility. He housed himself and his entourage in the seedy Hotel Theresa at the corner of 125th Street and 7th Avenue in Harlem, one of New York City's poorest neighborhoods. He used the hotel as the venue for his first meeting with the leader of the Soviet Union, Premier Nikita Khrushchev. When Castro met the short, stout Russian leader at the door of the hotel on September 20 and embraced him, he caused an outraged uproar in the U.S. press.[5]

That same afternoon, Khrushchev publicly embraced Castro on the floor of the UN General Assembly. Bolstered by the dramatic gesture of Soviet support, Castro gave an angry four-and-a-half-hour speech before the Assembly, bitterly denouncing the United States and accusing the U.S. government of sponsoring "aggression" against his country.

On October 13, President Eisenhower banned all American exports to Cuba, with the exception of some essential foods and medicines. Castro responded by seizing American businesses, including the Cuban operations of Coca-Cola and Sears, Roebuck. On December 16, shortly before the end of his term in office, an exasperated Eisenhower finally

Castro's four-and-a-half-hour
speech at the United Nations
included a bitter denunciation
of the United States.

ordered American imports of Cuban sugar cut to zero.

As the troubled year of 1960 drew to a close, the atmosphere within Cuba was that of a country under siege. Opposition groups set off bombs nightly in Cuban cities, Cuban exile pilots flew air raids against Cuban targets from bases in Florida, and anti-Castro guerrillas staged raids from the Sierra de Trinidad. Rumors flew about the island about the invasion force being trained in the United States. As 1961 dawned, Cubans braced themselves to meet the attack they knew must come sooner or later.

At 6:00 A.M. on Sunday, April 15, 1961, American B-26 bombers attacked several Cuban air force bases. The planes, piloted by Cuban exiles, were painted with Cuban markings to make it appear as if Castro's own air force was rising up against him. Castro, however, had assumed that an air attack would precede an invasion and had dispersed his aircraft. Nine of his planes survived.

The next day, in a speech given at the funeral of seven airmen killed in the raids, Castro nailed his colors to the mast. After months of denying publicly what everyone knew was true, he openly declared that his revolution was Communist. "Workers and peasants," he declared, "comrades, this is a socialist and democratic revolution of the poor, by the poor, and for the poor."[6]

Shortly before dawn on April 17, 1,400 Cuban exiles with tanks and artillery supplied by the United States began to land on two beaches in the narrow Bahía de Cochinos, or Bay of Pigs, 110 miles (180 kilometers) from Havana on Cuba's southern coast. Castro immediately ordered his remaining aircraft to attack the ships that had landed the invasion force. The planes sank two freighters, damaged the CIA command ship, and forced the rest of the fleet to flee, leaving 1,300 men stranded on the beaches.

Within twenty-four hours, Castro had an army of 20,000 men surrounding the Bay of Pigs. The new American president, John F. Kennedy, was reluctant to have American forces drawn into the fighting and refused to authorize strikes by the U.S. Air Force. By the evening of April 19, the commander of the exiles realized that his situation was hopeless. He ordered his men to escape as best they could; 1,189 of them were eventually captured.

The spectacular victory at the Bay of Pigs raised Castro's popularity in Cuba to new heights. He had done what generations of Cubans had only dreamed of: He had stood up to the United States and had won.

For most Cubans in the euphoric days that followed the victory all was well—as long as Castro ruled it did not matter that he was a Communist. A popular song called *Cuba Sí, Yanquis No* (*Cuba Yes, Yankees No*) captured the confidence that the Cuban public had in its new leader:

Si las cosas de Fidel
son cosas de buen marxista
que me pongan en la lista
que estoy de acuerdo con el.

If Fidel's concerns
are those of a good Marxist,
put me down on the list,
for I agree with him.[7]

8

Charting His Own Course

Castro fully expected the United States to mount a second invasion of Cuba, this time using American troops. In the months that followed the Bay of Pigs, he stepped up his efforts to secure Soviet military aid. To convince the Soviets that he was serious about communism, he announced in June 1961 the merger of the PSP, M-26-7, and the Revolutionary Directorate into the *Organizaciones Integradas Revolucionarias* (Integrated Revolutionary Organization), or OIR. This was the first step in Cuba's transformation into a Soviet-style single-party state.

Despite his desire for Soviet assistance, Castro remained wary of relying too much on Moscow. He did not want Cuba to exchange its former dependence on the United States for a similar dependence on the Soviet Union.

Castro believed that for Cuba's ultimate independence the island had to be made economically self-sufficient. To achieve this end, he embarked on a massive reorganization of the Cuban economy, discouraging sugar cultivation in favor of food crops, and launching a crash program of industrialization. He appointed Che Guevara as Cuba's minister of industry. Guevara set up a system of centralized economic planning in which the government took control of factory budgets and production targets.

As part of his development campaign, Castro tried to extend the guerrilla discipline of the Sierra Maestra to Cuban society as a whole. Calling for the creation of a "New Man,"[1] he encouraged Cubans to adopt the virtues of austerity, hard work, and public-spiritedness. In speech after speech he asked his audiences to give up their private desires and pitch in to create a truly independent Cuba in which the necessities of life would be available to everyone.

Castro cracked down hard on opposition to his policies. Police arrested thousands of dissenters on charges of spreading "counter-revolutionary influences." In every neighborhood the government set up a Committee for the Defense of the Revolution. These committees were given the task of observing any suspicious behavior or criticism of the government and reporting it to the authorities.

As the crackdown took hold, neighbor began to distrust neighbor, and fear of the government spread through Cuban society. Opponents of the regime who had enough money fled the country to join the exile community in the United States. Others went underground or, unable to escape the police, languished in government prisons.

WHILE CASTRO was working to make Cuba economically independent, his growing military relationship with the Soviet Union suddenly threatened to place

Cuba at the center of a world war. Sometime during the spring of 1962, Soviet Premier Khrushchev conceived the idea of basing Soviet medium-range nuclear missiles in Cuba as part of his struggle for global power with the United States. The plan promised to change the international balance of power in favor of the Soviet Union by placing nuclear missiles where they could hit American cities with little or no warning.

Pleased by the prospect of a greater Soviet military commitment to his regime, Castro agreed to Khrushchev's proposal. By October 1962, Soviet ships had delivered twenty missiles and warheads, along with 40,000 Soviet troops to protect them.[2] When photographs taken from an American U-2 spy plane revealed the presence of the missiles in Cuba, however, an outraged President Kennedy demanded their withdrawal. Kennedy followed the demand by imposing a quarantine line 500 miles (805 kilometers) from the Cuban coast. Soviet ships that tried to cross the line, he declared, would be fired on by the U.S. Navy.[3]

The world held its breath as Khrushchev and Kennedy tested each other's nerve. Neither man seemed ready to back down. On October 24, a Soviet convoy carrying twenty more warheads neared the U.S. quarantine line with no sign of hesitation. Aboard American warships, sailors and pilots prepared for battle. All-out war between the two superpowers seemed inevitable.

At the last moment, the Soviet fleet turned around. Over the next week, Khrushchev and Kennedy negotiated an end to the crisis. Khrushchev eventually agreed to remove all Soviet missiles from

A U.S. Defense Department photograph, taken at the height of the Cuban missile crisis, shows a Soviet missile site in western Cuba.

Cuba in exchange for an American promise never to invade the island.

Castro heard about the end of the crisis from the Associated Press. He was furious at having been left out of the negotiations, feeling that both he and Cuba had been used as pawns in the conflict between superpowers. According to Che Guevara, when the news arrived Castro screamed curses and kicked the wall.[4] To take revenge on Khrushchev, Castro refused to allow United Nations inspectors to enter Cuba to verify the missiles' withdrawal. UN supervision had been a key provision of the U.S.-Soviet agreement.

Cuba's economic situation made it impossible for Castro to maintain his posture of independence for long. His grand scheme for making the country self-sufficient was not working. Cuban farmers, used to growing sugarcane, and crippled by the flight of the country's best agricultural experts into exile, could not grow enough food to meet the island's needs. Imported Soviet industrial equipment proved incompatible with Cuba's mostly American-built factories, while Soviet technicians sent to train Cuban workers could not match the competence of their American counterparts. By March 1962, Cuba's industrial and agricultural production had fallen so low that the government was forced to begin rationing nearly all consumer goods.

By 1963, Castro and his advisers had to admit that their plans had been unrealistic. Che Guevara later remarked, "We did not base our arguments on statistical facts, nor on historical experience. We dealt with nature . . . as if by talking to it we could persuade it."[5] The Cuban people had given their all, but had been stopped by the cold facts of economic reality. Guevara's Ministry of Industry was dismantled and government resources were diverted from industry back into sugar production.

ALTHOUGH HE HAD FAILED to make Cuba self-sufficient, Castro did not give up on his dream of securing the island's independence. To reach his

MAYOR PRODUCCION
A MENOS COSTO

1964
AÑO DELA
ECONOMIA

After Castro's effort to make Cuba self-sufficient failed, the focus returned to sugar production. This huge government sign names 1964 as the "year of the economy" and offers the slogan "greater production at less cost."

goal, he needed to find support from nations aligned with neither the Soviet Union nor the United States.

Throughout the 1960s, just such a group, called the Non-Aligned Movement, had in fact been taking shape. It was made up mostly of Third World nations in Africa, Asia, and Latin America, many of which had just emerged or were struggling to break free from European colonial rule.

As early as 1959, Castro had sent weapons, medical supplies, and military advisers to help rebel movements in Africa. After the failure of his industrialization campaign he extended his support for Third World revolutions to include guerrilla movements in Peru, Guatemala, Colombia, and Venezuela. Castro hoped that by helping these revolutions to succeed he could begin to build a worldwide network of pro-Cuban governments that would help him reduce his dependence on the Soviet Union.

Castro's support for Third World revolution won Cuba increasing prestige within the Non-Aligned Movement. This was reflected by the choice of Havana to host the Tri-Continental Congress of Third World nations in January 1966. Castro's policies angered the Soviets, however, who felt that political organization, strikes, and elections—not revolution—would best ensure Communist victory in the Third World. Castro refused to be cowed. In his speech to open the conference, he publicly proclaimed that any revolutionary movement anywhere in the world could count on Cuba's help.[6]

Moscow reacted to Castro's waywardness by cutting back on its shipments of oil and gasoline to Cuba and by delaying the signing of important trade

Castro, visiting the Soviet Union in 1964, toured factories with Nikita Khrushchev. Despite promises of friendship, relations between the two countries became strained.

agreements with Castro's government. A furious Castro responded by refusing to attend celebrations held in the fall of 1967 in the Soviet Union to mark the fiftieth anniversary of the Russian Revolution.

Castro's hopes to base Cuban independence on support from the Third World were soon dashed. The guerrilla movements in Latin America on which he had counted gradually collapsed. In October 1967, Che Guevara was killed by American-trained Bolivian Rangers in Bolivia, where he was trying to build a new guerrilla army. Guevara's death dealt a deep personal blow to Castro and shattered the invincible image of the veterans of the Sierra Maestra.

Despite the failure of many of his policies, Castro still enjoyed broad support in Cuba. His popularity rested primarily on his charisma and on his consummate skill as a speechmaker. Cubans loved Castro's thundering denunciations of his enemies and delighted in his manner of alternating statistics about the economy with homespun examples. In one popular speech to a group of metalworkers in 1967, for example, Castro used the famous Cuban Coppelia ice cream to argue that goods produced by a state-run, socialist economy were superior to those made in the competitive free market.[7]

Castro's devotion to the tasks of government also contributed to his popularity among ordinary Cubans. He rejected the luxurious lifestyle common to prerevolutionary Cuban leaders, preferring to travel about the country involving himself in local affairs. Many Cubans came to regard Castro as their personal comrade and benefactor. With the help of a steady stream of praise from the government-run television and print media, an almost religious cult of personality gradually developed around the man whom people had come to call the *Lider Maximo*, the "Maximum Leader."

No amount of personal charm and hard work, however, could conceal the fact that Cuba's economy was still in serious trouble. Crippled by poor planning and a lack of technical skill, and by the continuing slowdown in oil shipments from the Soviet Union, Cuban farms and factories could not satisfy the demand for consumer goods. Cubans still had to endure food rationing. Even such ordinary items as light bulbs, shoelaces, and writing paper were hard to find. The Revolution's failure to fulfill its promise of a good standard of living for all caused increasing public dissatisfaction, even among those most loyal to Castro.

Part of the problem lay with Castro himself. His insistence on direct involvement with projects at the local level and his tendency to rapidly shift his enthusiasm from one project to the next made it difficult for government planners to implement consistent economic policies. Castro, however, believed that Cuba's economic woes were due to a lack of discipline among the population. He was particularly annoyed by the manner in which small farmers and traders took advantage of rationing to run a thriving black market. He commented angrily, "We did not make a revolution in order to establish the right to trade."[8]

In March 1968, Castro launched a "Revolutionary Offensive" to wipe out the last vestiges of free enterprise in Cuba. He nationalized 55,000 of the country's remaining small businesses, not even sparing the vendors who sold fried-egg sandwiches from tiny stands in the streets of Havana. In his speeches he hammered again and again on the theme of discipline as the route to national salvation. In an address in September to representatives of the Committees for the Defense of the Revolution he declared, "No liberalism! No softening! A revolutionary nation, an organized nation, a combative nation, a strong nation, because these are the virtues that are required these days."9

IN 1969, CASTRO decided to try one last spectacular throw of the dice to save the Cuban economy. Proclaiming a "Year of Decisive Endeavor," he called on Cubans to produce an unprecedented sugar harvest of ten million tons. Such a harvest would enable Cuba to pay off its foreign debt and buy Castro the economic and political independence he craved.

Castro staked his personal reputation and that of his regime on the success of the harvest. On October 18, 1969, he proclaimed, "The ten million ton harvest represents far more than tons of sugar, far more than an economic victory; it is a test, a moral commitment for this country. . . . Ten million tons less a single pound—we declare it before all the world—will be a defeat, not a victory."10

The entire Cuban population was drawn into the effort. Workers, students, children, and even foreigners joined the professional *macheteros* (cane cutters) to harvest sugarcane. Castro extended the harvest season, which normally lasted from December to February, until July 1970, to handle the increased yield, and postponed all holidays, including Christmas. To set a personal example, he himself worked in the fields cutting cane for four hours every day. By the spring of 1970, however, it became clear that the massive effort had failed. The harvest eventually fell 1.5 million tons short of its goal.

On July 26, 1970, the seventeenth anniversary of the Moncada assault, Castro rose before a huge crowd and took full responsibility both for the failure to reach ten million tons and for all of the failures of his regime during the past decade. "We are going to begin," he said, "by pointing out the responsibility of all of [the leaders] and mine in particular for all these problems."[11] He even went so far as to make an offer to resign, which few people took seriously and which was loyally shouted down by the crowd.

Castro now faced a challenge as great as the one he had faced when he set out to overthrow Batista with a handful of men. The sugar harvest had failed to break Cuba's dependence on the Soviet Union. If Castro was to lead Cuba to development and independence, he had to find a new path.

9

On the World Stage

The sugar campaign of 1969–1970 left the Cuban economy in worse shape than before. Loyally responding to Castro's call, half a million workers had left their jobs to go to work in the sugar fields, bringing the rest of Cuba's already weak production system to a halt. Frustrated and disillusioned by the campaign's failure to bring the promised prosperity, many Cubans simply stopped showing up for work; in August and September 1970, as many as 20 percent of the country's workers were absent from their jobs. It was clear to everyone that patriotic slogans and free government services were no longer an adequate substitute for goods in the stores.

The crisis left Castro with little choice but to turn to the Soviet Union for help. Reluctantly, he allowed Soviet experts into Cuba to begin the task of rebuilding the island's shattered economy. Under Soviet guidance, Cuban planners evolved a new system of economic management for the island. Control from Havana was loosened to allow the directors of factories and farms greater decision-making power. Managers were ordered to try to make a profit instead of meeting government production targets at any cost. In the most radical break with the past, Cuban workers were given incentives, such as overtime pay and production bonuses, to increase their productivity.

In 1972, Cuba formally applied to join the Council for Mutual Economic Assistance (COMECON), the economic community of Communist nations. The COMECON system filled the needs of the Communist world by encouraging member countries to produce only those products for which they were best suited. COMECON membership guaranteed Cuba trade with the Soviet Union and its Eastern European allies. At the same time, it locked Cuba into the dependence on sugar that Castro had struggled so hard to overturn.

The new economic system increased the efficiency of farms and factories and protected local planners from Castro's well-intentioned but often disastrous meddling. Cuba's return to Soviet favor renewed the flow of oil and other essential goods from the Socialist bloc. As a result, the Cuban economy gradually began to recover.

While Soviet and Cuban experts labored to rebuild the island's economy, Cuban politicians took similar steps to decentralize the government and allow local leaders a greater role in political decision making. Their reforms were embodied in a new constitution that, on the surface, appeared to guarantee the Cuban people democracy. The constitution provided for government by a president and a Council of State and created the *Organos del Poder Popular*, or

People's Power Apparatus. The People's Power Apparatus allowed the Cuban people to elect their own local assemblies for the first time since the Revolution. These assemblies elected delegates to Provincial Assemblies, which in turn elected the members of the National Assembly. The National Assembly was given the power to review and approve all new laws. Under the new constitution, which won approval in a nationwide referendum in early 1976 by 97.7 percent of the vote,[1] Castro became president of Cuba. He kept his position as commander in chief of the Cuban armed forces.

Despite the appearance of democracy, the constitution of 1976 left all real political power in Cuba concentrated at the top. This was due to the dominant role played by the Cuban Communist party, which had been formed from the OIR in 1965. Anyone who wished to hold a prominent position in the government had to be a member of the party. As a result, the party came to dominate the government bureaucracy and later, after the approval of the constitution, the National Assembly and the Council of State.

The party's central governing body, the Political Bureau or "Politburo," kept party members under strict discipline and enforced obedience to the party line. The Politburo, therefore, along with the Communist-dominated Council of State, determined government policy. The National Assembly became a rubber-stamp body that met only a few days each year to discuss and pass legislation already approved by Communist leaders.

Castro recognized the leading role of the Communist party in a speech at the party's First Congress in 1975. He declared before the assembled delegates, "The party is everything . . . it is the party that makes the ideas, the principles, and the forces of the revolution a reality."[2]

As Castro gradually gave up direct control of Cuban internal affairs, he turned his attention more and more to foreign policy. In this arena, unfettered by any restrictions, he could still pursue his dream of Cuban independence.

Castro's support during the 1960s for armed revolution had alienated many Latin American governments. After 1970, in an effort to end his isolation in the region, Castro began for the first time to acknowledge publicly that elections as well as guerrilla uprisings could bring freedom and justice to the people of Latin America.

Events in Chile gave Castro a perfect opportunity to display his new image. In 1970, the handsome Marxist politician Salvador Allende, a longtime friend of Castro's, ran for the Chilean presidency and won. Allende became the head of the first socialist government in Latin America to take power in a free election.

In November 1971, Castro made a state visit to Chile. During the visit he hailed Allende's victory and called for the creation of a community of Latin American nations that would support each other economically. Despite his public enthusiasm, Castro remained uncertain about the safety of elected socialist regimes in a hemisphere dominated by the United States. When the Chilean army, backed by the CIA, deposed Allende in September 1973 and installed the pro-American General Augusto Pinochet as Chile's president, an angry Castro warned a mass

Castro and Chilean president Allende in 1971. When right-wing forces deposed the socialist Allende in 1973, Castro warned of the need for vigilance.

rally in Cuba about the need for vigilance. "The Chilean example," he declared, "teaches us the lesson that it is impossible to make the revolution with the people alone: arms are also necessary! And that arms alone aren't enough to make a revolution: people are necessary."[3]

Castro's new moderate approach toward Latin America paid off. In December 1972, the Caribbean island nations of Barbados, Jamaica, Guyana, and Trinidad defied the Organization of American States (OAS), which had expelled Cuba in 1962, and opened formal diplomatic relations with Castro's regime. Shortly afterward, Cuba was allowed to join several organizations devoted to Latin American development.

As a second step in his foreign policy offensive, Castro reluctantly tried to improve his relations with the United States. By 1975, relations had improved to the point where the United States, taking note of the improved diplomatic atmosphere in Latin America, voted with the majority of OAS members to lift the organization's economic sanctions against Cuba.

WHILE THINGS WERE IMPROVING for Cuba in the Western Hemisphere, Castro had his share of trouble in the rest of the world. His enforced surrender to the Soviet Union in the wake of the sugar harvest of 1969–1970 badly damaged his reputation as an independent champion of the Non-Aligned Movement. By 1973, when the leaders of the Non-Aligned nations met in a summit meeting in the North African city of Algiers, Castro's standing had fallen so low that some members questioned Cuba's right to remain in the movement.

Events in Africa, however, gave Castro an opportunity to redeem himself in the eyes of the Third World. On October 14, 1975, South Africa, with U.S. approval, launched a sudden invasion of the Portuguese colony of Angola in southwest Africa. Angola was scheduled to become independent of Portugal in November; the South African invasion was designed to destroy the socialist Popular Movement for the Liberation of Angola (MPLA), the most popular of three guerrilla movements jockeying to take control of the country after the Portuguese withdrawal. The other two movements, the National Front for the Liberation of Angola (FNLA) and the National Union for the Total Independence of Angola (UNITA), had the backing of the United States.

Castro had long supported the MPLA with weapons and military advisers. When news of the South African attack reached him, he instantly ordered a massive air- and sea-lift of 20,000 Cuban troops to Angola.

At his happiest in the middle of a war, Castro threw himself into the operation. Each departure of a ship loaded with troops for Angola found the Maximum Leader at the dockside giving a rousing pep talk to his men. Gabriel García Márquez, a Colombian writer who observed Castro during the war, later wrote that in the early phases of the conflict, "Castro remained up to fourteen hours straight in the operations room of the general staff, at times without eating or sleeping, as if he were in the battlefield himself. He followed the details of every battle with colored pins on the detailed maps which covered the walls, and remained in constant communication with the top commands of the MPLA. . . ."[4]

The first Cuban troops to arrive in Angola helped the MPLA successfully defend the country's capital, Luanda. By the end of November, Cuban and MPLA forces had turned the tide, sending the South Africans and their guerrilla allies back in full retreat. By February 1976, the MPLA had gained control of most of Angola.

Although the MPLA had regained the upper hand in Angola, it was Castro who had scored the real triumph. His intervention received widespread praise in the Third World, wiping out Cuba's image as a lackey of the Soviet Union and raising Castro up once more as a champion of the Non-Aligned Movement. A Non-Aligned summit meeting in Sri Lanka in the summer of 1976 officially endorsed Castro's action, and named Havana to host the next Non-Aligned summit, which was scheduled for 1979.

The Angolan war also gave a boost to Castro's popularity in Cuba. Cubans forgot the economic disaster of 1969–1970 in a surge of pride at the accomplishments of their army. Many saw the victory as proof of the strength and vitality of the Revolution, and as a glorious symbol of Cuba's newfound role as a world power.

At the beginning of the Angolan crisis, the United States angrily threatened to break off its negotiations with Cuba unless Castro removed his troops. Castro indignantly refused, asserting his right to make foreign policy of his own without being dictated to by Washington.

After the Cuban victory, however, the United States agreed to resume talks. The negotiations resulted in the creation of "interest sections" in Havana and Washington, the first step toward the reestablishment of formal diplomatic relations.

The dialogue between the United States and Cuba came to an abrupt halt in 1977 when Castro, at the request of the Soviet Union, sent 15,000 Cuban troops to the East African nation of Ethiopia. The Soviets wanted Castro to help the Ethiopians resist an invasion by neighboring Somalia, which had the support of the United States.

Castro's involvement in Ethiopia had very different results than his intervention in Angola. Many members of the Non-Aligned Movement saw his action as renewed evidence that he danced to the Soviet tune. As a result, his position in the movement plummeted.

Events in the spring and summer of 1979, however, once again put Castro in the spotlight. In March, a revolution on the tiny eastern Caribbean island of Grenada brought a pro-Cuban socialist leader, Maurice Bishop, to power. The following July, the *Sandinista* guerrilla movement in Nicaragua, which Castro had trained and armed, succeeded in overthrowing the brutal dictatorship of Nicaraguan strongman Anastasio Somoza. The sudden appearance of two new socialist states in Latin America strengthened Cuba's position in the region and seemed to justify Castro's long belief in the power of armed revolution.

Three months after the Sandinista victory, in September 1979, Castro hosted the Sixth Conference of the Non-Aligned Movement. Ninety-two Third World leaders or their representatives gathered in Havana to map out a common course for the future. The delegates elected Castro to serve as the chairman of the movement for the next four years, bringing him the official leadership of the Third World and the power that he had craved for so long.

Castro's 1979 speech to the United Nations included calls for Puerto Rican statehood and a condemnation of Israel.

One month later, Castro traveled to New York City for the first time in nineteen years. Where before he had come to the United Nations as the untried leader of a small island nation, now he came to address the UN General Assembly in his capacity as chairman of the Non-Aligned Movement. In his speech, which lasted for two hours, Castro called on the leaders of the rich and powerful nations of the world to grant money to end the hunger, ignorance, disease, and injustice that plagued the Third World.

The 1979 Non-Aligned Summit and the address before the United Nations marked the zenith of Castro's career. The Maximum Leader had taken his tiny island nation and turned it into a force to be reckoned with in world affairs. His personal popularity in Cuba stood at an all-time high, supported by the official Cuban press, which trumpeted his foreign successes.

Gone was the athletic young revolutionary dressed in combat fatigues with a cigar clenched between his teeth who had driven about the Cuban countryside in a jeep during the 1960s. Castro now appeared as a slightly overweight but dignified statesman with tinges of gray in his beard who appeared at important functions dressed in a medal-bedecked army uniform.

Yet Castro's successes as a statesman abroad only served to obscure the serious problems that faced him at home. Despite an improved supply of the basic necessities of life, Cuba's state-run economy was still failing to provide Cubans with the material standard of living that they sorely needed. Thousands of political prisoners languished in Cuban jails for opposing press censorship and Communist control of the government. A steady stream of refugees swelled the ranks of Cuban exile communities in Latin America and Florida. Castro's future as Cuba's leader depended on his ability to convince the Cuban people that, despite its weaknesses, his Revolution still held the best promise for their future welfare and happiness.

10

Socialism or Death!

On December 24, 1979, 30,000 Soviet troops invaded Afghanistan, a mountainous country in south central Asia bordered by Iran, Pakistan, the Soviet Union, and China. The Soviets were intervening to end a civil war that threatened to topple the pro-Soviet Afghan government.

The Soviet invasion of Afghanistan provoked a worldwide storm of criticism. The United Nations quickly voted to condemn the attack. In the United States, President Jimmy Carter placed an embargo on sales of American grain to the Soviet Union and withdrew the U.S. Olympic team from the 1980 Moscow Olympic Games.

The Afghanistan crisis placed Castro in a difficult position. Afghanistan had been a founding member of the Non-Aligned Movement. If Castro approved Soviet interference in the affairs of a Non-Aligned state, he risked losing his leadership of the movement. If he criticized Moscow, however, he could lose the Soviet economic and military aid on which Cuba's survival depended.

In the end, Castro went with the Soviet Union. He ordered Cuba's representative to the United Nations to vote against the resolution condemning the Soviet action. In the storm of criticism in the Third World that followed, Castro kept his post as chairman of the Non-Aligned Movement but lost the seat on the UN Security Council, the body that monitors and upholds world peace, that should have come to him with the position.[1]

A personal blow struck Castro shortly after the Afghanistan disaster. On January 11, 1980, his companion, confidante, and helpmate Celia Sánchez died of lung cancer. Celia's death devastated Castro. During the months that followed, many observers noticed that he seemed withdrawn and preoccupied at public functions. Others detected a slowing in the pace of government decision making, a clear sign of Castro's depression.[2]

In the spring and summer of 1980, events in Cuba shook Castro even further. In April, a group of Cubans hoping to gain political asylum in Peru crashed a truck through the gates of the Peruvian embassy in Havana. The Peruvian government honored the refugees' request for asylum and refused to hand them over to Cuban authorities.

Since the early 1960s, Castro had reached periodic agreements with the United States allowing people to leave Cuba to join family members who had fled the country. Such arrangements were to his advantage, because they served to rid the country of potential troublemakers. Most Cubans, however, with the exception of elderly people who could no longer work or serve in the military, were prohibited from receiving exit visas.

When he heard of the incident at the Peruvian embassy, an outraged Castro responded by withdrawing all Cuban guards from around the embassy and publicly announcing that any Cubans who wished to could leave the country. The response seriously embarrassed his regime. Ten thousand Cubans crowded into the Peruvian embassy and applied for asylum. To make matters worse, President Carter publicly declared that the United States would welcome any Cubans who wanted to start a new life in America.

Castro, bound by his own promise, could only watch as Cuban exiles living in Florida organized a sea-lift of refugees through the tiny Cuban port town of Mariel, 25 miles (40 kilometers) west of Havana. Thousands of small boats shuttled back and forth between Miami and Mariel to carry the crowds of Cubans who wanted to leave.

To counter the image that his government had lost all popular support, Castro organized large rallies of loyal Cubans. Crowds of faithful Fidelistas jeered the refugees as they boarded their boats in Mariel, calling them *gusanos*, "worms."[3] To take revenge on the United States, Castro ordered several thousand criminals and mental patients to be sent to Florida with the refugees.

The depth of the public discontent revealed by the Mariel boat-lift came as a severe shock to Castro. By the time the boat-lift ended in August, more than 120,000 Cubans had fled the island. Most of the refugees were working-class Cubans—the bedrock of the Revolution—unlike the intellectuals and professionals who had fled during the 1960s.

Shocked into action, Castro resorted to eco-

A commercial fishing boat overloaded with Cuban refugees heads toward Key West, Florida, in 1980.

nomic incentives to shore up his popularity. He authorized the government to lift rationing on many food items and to allow farmers to sell their surplus produce for profit at "free farmers markets." He also permitted the government to open state-run "parallel markets" in which Cubans could buy hard-to-find consumer goods at much higher prices.

In November 1980, former California governor Ronald Reagan defeated President Carter's bid for reelection and became president of the United States. The fervently anti-Communist Reagan quickly made it clear that he intended to deal harshly with Castro and his allies in the Caribbean. He tightened the U.S. economic embargo of Cuba and made it a condition of improved relations that Castro abandon his ties to the Soviet Union.

In the fall of 1983, Reagan demonstrated that he was prepared to use American military might against Communist governments in the region. On October 19, hard-line Marxist rebels in Grenada deposed and killed Castro's ally Maurice Bishop. Seizing the opportunity presented by the breakdown of law and order on the tiny island, Reagan authorized an American invasion of Grenada.

American troops landed in Grenada on October 25. Castro ordered the few hundred Cuban military advisers and construction workers on the island to fight to the last man. Although American soldiers tried their best to avoid contact with the Cubans, fighting was inevitable. In the first direct confrontation between U.S. and Cuban forces, the outnumbered Cubans were quickly overwhelmed; twenty-four men were killed and fifty-nine wounded.

On Grenada, Cuban prisoners march toward planes that will return them to their homeland.

The U.S. invasion of Grenada destroyed Castro's hopes of building an anti-American alliance among the island states of the Caribbean. In a burst of frustration, Castro demoted the survivors of the Cuban forces on Grenada for not obeying his orders to fight to the death.

FACED WITH the implacable hostility of the Reagan administration, Castro worked to rekindle support for his regime in the Third World. He seized upon the issue of Third World debt as an ideal propaganda tool. During the 1970s, Western nations had lent large sums of money to Third World countries with little concern for their ability to repay the loans. By the early 1980s the Third World debt had reached huge proportions; Latin American countries alone owed their creditors some $420 billion.

Castro began a public campaign to convince the rich nations of the West to cancel the Third World debt. By cutting their weapons budgets by as little as 12 percent, he argued, Western nations could not only cancel the debt but free up money to create a "new economic order" that would reduce the tremendous gap in living standards that separated the rich and the poor nations of the world.[4] Castro called on debtor nations to unite and use the threat of nonpayment of their debts to force the West to implement his plan.

This pragmatic strategy was a long way from Castro's early policy of uniting the Third World by exporting revolution. Castro expressed his change of heart in a speech to the Latin American Federation of Journalists in 1985: "I believe that the cancelation of debt and the establishment of the New International Economic Order is much more important than two, three or four isolated revolutions. . . . You can't meet the enormous needs that have accumulated in all our countries . . . with social changes alone."[5]

Castro's campaign found broad support, particularly in Latin America. As the region's renegade, Castro could freely express the frustration that many Latin Americans felt with their poverty and with their indebtedness to the West. His flamboyant speeches blasting the United States for its refusal to extend a helping hand to the Third World gained wide coverage in the world press, and contributed to a growing feeling among Latin American nations that they needed to unite to solve their common problems.

As Castro struggled to regain his prestige abroad, he found himself forced to turn his attention once more to Cuba's economy. Throughout the 1970s, the Cuban economy had steadily recovered from its low point following the sugar harvest of 1969–1970. In the early 1980s, however, bad weather, poor planning, and the tightened U.S. trade embargo sent the economy once more into a sharp decline. By 1983, Cuban sugar production had fallen so low that Castro had to buy sugar on the world market to meet his sales obligations to the Soviet Union.[6]

Cuba's economic downturn was accompanied by growing public anger. Many Cubans were frustrated by the lack of goods in the inexpensive state-run stores and resented the high prices charged in the better-stocked parallel markets. Government officials and high-ranking military officers also caused a great deal of resentment by taking advantage of shortages to make huge amounts of money on the parallel market, adding their profits to the privileges that came with government service to lead lives of luxury far beyond the reach of the average Cuban.

In February 1986, Castro rose before the Third Congress of the Cuban Communist party and announced a new domestic reform program that he solemnly called the "Rectification of Errors and Negative Trends." Adroitly placing himself on the side of the people, he denounced government corruption and severely criticized the entrepreneurs who had taken advantage of the policies of the 1970s to enrich themselves. He called for a return to the patriotic moral values of the early days of the Revolution, when Cubans had thought less of their own wants and more of the survival of the country.

The Rectification campaign rolled back many of the free market reforms of the 1970s and early 1980s. Central control of economic decision making was increased. The free farmers markets that the government had created in the wake of the Mariel crisis were closed. Thousands of economic managers and middle-ranking government officials lost their jobs as part of an effort to end corruption and make the bureaucracy more efficient.

Castro appealed to ordinary Cubans to give up their desires for luxuries and tighten their belts. Patriotic slogans posted on signs and buildings throughout the island called for Cubans to rally to the support of the Revolution. One such slogan captured the call to action with the phrase: *Socialismo o muerte*—"Socialism or Death!"[7]

IN 1985, SHORTLY BEFORE the beginning of the Rectification campaign, a young reform-minded leader named Mikhail Gorbachev came to power in the Soviet Union. Gorbachev faced many of the same problems that Castro did: a weak economy, an inefficient government bureaucracy, and widespread frustration on the part of ordinary Soviet citizens.

Gorbachev, however, took a very different approach to solving these problems. He set in motion a reform program described by the two Russian words *perestroika* and *glasnost*. *Perestroika* ("restructuring") involved a drastic weakening of central government control over the economy to tap the energies of the free market. *Glasnost* ("openness") aimed to shake up the bureaucracy by encouraging public criticism of the government.

Glasnost and *perestroika* resembled in many respects the Cuban reform program of the 1970s. Castro himself was quick to point out the similarities. In a 1988 interview with the American television network NBC he declared, "We have *glasnost* here, we have always had it. No party in the world has been more self-critical than the Communist party of Cuba."[8]

Yet the reforms taking place in the Soviet Union were much more far reaching than those that Castro had permitted. In Cuba, criticism was only allowed within the limits of the Communist system. No one could criticize the Revolution itself or its ideals. In the Soviet Union, on the other hand, a wide-ranging public debate, encouraged by Gorbachev, was taking shape on the very future of communism itself.

Gorbachev's rise to power in the Soviet Union heralded a new and dangerous era for Cuba. To lessen the drain on the Soviet economy by the huge Soviet military establishment, Gorbachev pulled back from the traditional Soviet policy of supporting socialism abroad. He also began to work for an end to the Soviet Union's long Cold War with the United States.

In a visit to Cuba in April 1989, Gorbachev made it clear that he intended to change the Soviet Union's relationship with Cuba to conform with his new policies. In a speech to the Cuban National Assembly, the Soviet leader declared, "As life moves ahead, new demands are being made on the quality of our interaction."9 The Soviet Union would no longer support Cuba at any cost. Trade between the two countries would in the future be based on profitability rather than politics, while military aid would be restricted by the demands of the new U.S.-Soviet relationship.

As the 1980s drew to a close, Castro faced an uncertain future. The Soviet Union was distancing itself from his regime while the United States remained as hostile as ever. He remained a popular figure at home, but his government faced increasing public discontent. Far from having made his Revolution secure, Castro confronted a battle for its survival as difficult as any in its thirty-year history.

11

Going It Alone

In 1989 the nations of Eastern Europe, encouraged by the changes sweeping the Soviet Union, abandoned communism and freed themselves from Soviet control. In a matter of months the entire structure of Soviet world power came tumbling down. Castro suddenly found himself without his secure place in the COMECON, which for all practical purposes had ceased to exist.

Events in the Western Hemisphere left Castro even more isolated. On December 20, 1989, American forces invaded Panama, deposing Castro's friend and supporter General Manuel Antonio Noriega and taking him to the United States to stand trial on charges of drug trafficking. Two months later, on February 25, 1990, the Sandinistas in Nicaragua suffered a stunning defeat in nationwide elections and lost control of the Nicaraguan government.

With Castro's international support disappearing, the United States took an even harder line against him. In March 1990, President George Bush, who succeeded Ronald Reagan in 1988, stiffened the requirements for an improvement in U.S.-Cuban relations. Bush declared that Cuba had to hold free, democratic, and internationally supervised elections, adopt a free-market economy, and cut the size of its armed forces before the United States would come to the negotiating table.[1]

The cutback in Soviet economic aid and the collapse of the COMECON had a devastating effect in Cuba. Rationing increased to include even ordinary goods such as tobacco, soap, and cooking oil. A serious shortage of oil and gasoline threatened to immobilize factories and farm machinery. A lack of spare parts from Eastern Europe made many of Havana's Hungarian-built city buses useless and threatened to slow down the island's all-important sugar harvest by disabling harvesting machines.

Castro met the crisis by ordering a "Special Period in Peacetime." The order set in motion plans designed to see Cuba through the hardships of a major war. Factories not producing critical products were closed to save fuel. The government moved thousands of city dwellers to the countryside to work on farms and help increase food production. Farm tractors idled by lack of spare parts and fuel were replaced by machines drawn by horses and oxen. Thousands of bicycles were imported from China to replace city buses and taxis.

At the same time, Castro began warning Cubans to prepare themselves for what he called the "Zero Option"—the suspension of all food and oil shipments from the Soviet Union. Cuba's dependence on the trickle of Soviet aid that remained was made starkly clear in January 1991 when the late arrival of a single ship carrying grain and flour from the Soviet Union forced the government to cut bread rations and to sharply raise the price of eggs.[2]

Castro tried to rally the Cuban people to endure the hardship by appealing to their patriotism. He blamed the United States for the crisis and vowed to continue fighting for the survival of the Revolution. At a summit meeting of the Latin American heads of state in the summer of 1991 he defiantly declared, "We [Cubans] are preparing ourselves economically, preparing ourselves politically, preparing ourselves morally and preparing ourselves militarily. . . . What are we going to do? Anything is possible except that Cuba should raise the white flag."[3]

In August 1991, Castro's worst nightmare came true. Conservative Communists in the Soviet Union who opposed President Gorbachev's reforms briefly seized control of the government with the aid of hard-liners in the Soviet military. The Soviet people, however, refused to give up their new-found freedoms. Crowds took to the streets of Moscow, led by one of the Soviet Union's most ardent reformers, President Boris Yeltsin of Russia, and forced the plotters to abandon their attempt to take over the government.

The failure of the coup attempt in the Soviet Union spelled the end for Soviet aid to Cuba. The Soviet central government began to disintegrate. Many conservative officials who had favored continued support for Castro fell from power. The governments of the individual Soviet republics, many of which were led by men like Yeltsin who wanted to cut all aid to Cuba, began to assert their independence.

In September, President Gorbachev, his power drastically weakened and his country coming apart around him, signaled the end of Soviet economic and military aid to Cuba. He announced that the Soviet Union would no longer subsidize its trade with Cuba and that 11,000 Soviet troops would shortly leave the island.

The following month, the Fourth Congress of the Cuban Communist party convened in Havana. The Congress turned into a contest between conservative Communists and a growing number of mainly younger party members who admired Gorbachev's reforms in the Soviet Union and wanted to apply them to Cuba.

Castro had no intention, however, of allowing Cuba to follow in the path of the Soviet Union. He was well aware that Gorbachev's liberal reforms had unleashed the popular forces that had overthrown communism in Eastern Europe and were destroying the Soviet Union itself. Although he agreed to a number of minor reforms (such as permitting the Cuban people to vote directly for members of the National Assembly), Castro insisted that the Communist party retain its control of the government and economy.

In a speech before the assembled delegates to the Congress, Castro vowed that Cuba would continue on its socialist course. "We are going to defend ourselves alone, surrounded by an ocean of capitalism," he declared defiantly. "Our greatest historical responsibility is the fight for our ideas, which is the fight of all the exploited, subjugated, hungry people of the world. They are not simply ideas. They are our destiny, our independence, our revolution."[4]

Despite the worldwide collapse of Communism, Castro remained a committed Marxist. Here the aging Cuban leader speaks beneath a statue of José Martí.

Castro continued to suppress public opposition. To back up the Committees for the Defense of the Revolution, which continued to watch every Cuban neighborhood and report antigovernment behavior to the police, he created "Rapid Response Brigades." These gangs of government supporters had orders to break up any public protests and to harass people who spoke out against the government.[5]

In an effort to salvage Cuba's crumbling economy, Castro continued efforts begun in late 1990 to attract foreign businesses to Cuba and to revive Cuba's tourist industry, which had largely vanished after the Revolution. The government set up special zones around Cuba's most attractive beaches and tourist attractions where foreigners could freely spend their money on overpriced items not available in the rest of the country. The government declared these "green zones" off limits to ordinary Cubans, causing a great deal of local resentment.

In July 1992, Castro made his first trip to Spain to take part in a meeting of Spanish and Latin American leaders and to lobby for new trade agreements. He found to his surprise that the tide of democracy that was sweeping the world had left him isolated. Crowds of protesters greeted him in Madrid. The socialist prime minister of Spain, Felipe González, gave him a frosty reception. His fellow Latin American leaders, instead of offering support, urged him to move Cuba toward democracy.[6]

The following month, President Carlos Salinas de Grotari of Mexico met with Jorge Mas Canosa, a millionaire Cuban-American businessman and head of the Cuban-American National Foundation, a powerful Cuban exile lobbying group devoted to

Castro's overthrow. The meeting was a sign that Mexico, one of the three wealthiest countries in Latin America and a traditional supporter of Cuba, had begun to distance itself from Castro's regime.

WITH HIS SUPPORT in the rest of the world dwindling as the 1990s progressed, Castro faced the problem of keeping his Revolution alive. Despite his crackdown on the opposition, public dissatisfaction in Cuba continued to grow. Cubans who had grown up since the Revolution had no memories of the horrors of the Batista regime and had learned to take the social benefits of Castroism for granted. They were less willing than their parents to endure the hardship of life in Castro's Cuba and craved the political freedom and higher standard of living available in the United States. Trying to bypass government travel restrictions, thousands of young men and women fled Cuba on makeshift rafts and rubber tires in an effort to reach Florida. According to the U.S. Coast Guard, many died in the dangerous Straits of Florida without reaching their goal.7

The United States showed no sign of giving up its efforts to overthrow Castro. Although many American moderates argued that Washington should relax its embargo on Cuban trade to deprive Castro of the ability to blame the United States for Cuba's problems, the U.S. government tightened its embargo further. In mid-1991, prodded by Canosa's Cuban-American National Foundation, the Bush administration limited the amount of money that Cuban exiles could send to their families in Cuba. In September 1992, Congress passed the Cuban Democracy Act, which forbade foreign subsidiaries of American companies to trade with Cuba and prohibited ships stopping in Cuba from unloading in U.S. ports.[8]

American officials in the early 1990s confidently asserted that Castro's fall was inevitable. They pointed to Cuba's disintegrating economy and the heroic escapes from the island as signs that Castro was losing his grip on power. Each year, with growing confidence, the Cuban exile community in Florida excitedly prepared for "Christmas in Havana."[9]

Yet Castro continued to draw on large reserves of support. Many older Cubans still remembered the injustice and corruption of the Batista dictatorship. They feared that the return of the Cuban exiles from the United States would bring a return of the Cuba of the 1950s. In addition, a large segment of the Cuban population still venerated Castro for his long and often lonely battle to keep Cuba free from American influence.

Castro could also point to some considerable achievements. As a result of his literacy campaign, Cuba boasted the highest percentage of people who could read and write of any country in the Third World. Castro's health care system, which guaranteed every Cuban free medical care, had also achieved impressive results. Although crippled by a lack of medical supplies since the cutoff of Soviet aid, the system gave Cubans the longest average life expectancy (seventy-six years) in the Third World. Cuba's infant death rate had fallen until it rivaled that of the wealthiest nations of the West.[10]

Most Cubans took for granted the free housing and education and the guaranteed income that Castro's regime provided. Many looked with fear toward Eastern Europe and the republics of the former

Soviet Union, where the end of communism threw as much as 40 percent of the population out of work.[11]

Castro himself, in his mid-sixties, was beginning to show signs of the strain of his battle for political survival. His famous beard had gone gray, and deep lines marked his once boyish face. Many ordinary Cubans, even Castro's most faithful supporters, began to say that it was time for the *Lider Maximo* to retire. Castro seemed at times prepared to admit that his resignation might benefit Cuba. In February 1993, in an interview with the American television network ABC, Castro suggested that if the price for the United States to lift its thirty-one-year-old trade embargo of Cuba was his departure from power, he would be ready to negotiate this with Washington.

If Castro were to step down, his brother Raúl would succeed him. A quiet man and a Communist hard-liner, Raúl always stood in his flamboyant brother's shadow. He has never commanded the affection and respect that the Cuban people have shown Fidel. Part of the reason for Castro's refusal to give up power may be the knowledge that only he can ask the people who have remained in Cuba to endure the hardships necessary to keep the Revolution alive. Whatever his future, however, Fidel Castro has changed forever the face of Cuba and the world.

Chronology

1926   Fidel Alejandro Castro Ruz is born near the village of Birán, in Oriente Province (August 13)

1941   Enters the Colegio de Belén in Havana

1945   Enters the University of Havana Law School

1947   Joins the Auténticos party; meets Eddy Chibás

1948   Marries Mirta Díaz-Balart (October 12)

1950   Graduates from the University of Havana with a Doctor of Law degree

1951   Eddy Chibás commits suicide (August 5); Castro runs for a seat in the Cuban Congress

1952   Fulgencio Batista seizes control of the Cuban government (March 10)

1953   Castro stages an abortive attack on the Moncada Barracks in Santiago de Cuba (July 26)

1955   Castro is released from prison as part of a general amnesty for political prisoners (May 7)
Flees to Mexico City after a government crackdown on the opposition (July 7) and forms the 26th of July Movement; meets Ernesto "Che" Guevara

1956   Lands in Cuba with eighty men in the yacht *Granma* (December 2); after the destruction of the expedition, retreats into the Sierra Maestra with the survivors to begin a guerrilla war

1957   Releases the Sierra Maestra Manifesto outlining his vision for a new Cuba (July 12)

1959   Batista flees Cuba (January 1); Castro enters Havana in triumph (January 8)
Castro becomes prime minister of Cuba (February); begins moving Communists into positions of power; forces Provisional President Manuel Urrutia to resign (July)

1960   U.S. president Dwight D. Eisenhower authorizes the CIA to train a force of Cuban exiles for an invasion of Cuba (March 17)
Castro establishes formal diplomatic relations with the Soviet Union (May 7)

1961   Cuban exile army lands at the Bay of Pigs in southwestern Cuba and is repelled by Cuban forces (April 17–19)

1962   Soviet ships carrying medium-range nuclear missiles arrive in Cuba, triggering the Cuban Missile Crisis (October)

1967   Che Guevara is killed leading a guerrilla movement in Bolivia (October)

1968   Castro launches the "Revolutionary Offensive" to wipe out the last vestiges of private enterprise in Cuba (March)

1969   "Year of Decisive Endeavor": Castro launches an unsuccessful campaign for a ten-million-ton sugar harvest to pay off Cuba's foreign debt and win Cuba's economic independence of the Soviet Union

1972   Cuba formally joins the Soviet-led Council for Mutual Economic Assistance (COMECON)

1975	Castro sends 20,000 Cuban troops to Angola
1976	New constitution permitting more local participation in government is ratified
1977	Castro sends 15,000 troops to Ethiopia
1979	Hosts the Sixth Conference of the Non-Aligned Movement in Havana (September)
1980	The Mariel boat-lift—more than 120,000 Cubans flee Castro's regime for the United States
1985	Mikhail Gorbachev comes to power in the Soviet Union, inaugurating a new period of liberalization
1986	Castro announces the "Rectification" campaign in an effort to revive Cuba's faltering economy (February)
1989	The nations of Eastern Europe renounce communism and break free from Soviet control
1990	Castro declares a "Special Period in Peacetime," implementing wartime economic austerity measures in an effort to keep the Cuban economy from collapsing (October)
1991	Fourth Congress of the Cuban Communist party convenes in Havana; Castro insists on keeping Cuba on a strict Communist path (October)
1992	U.S. Congress passes the Cuban Democracy Act tightening the U.S. economic embargo of Cuba

Notes

Chapter One

1. *Time,* January 19, 1959, p. 35.
2. Tad Szulc, *Fidel: A Critical Portrait* (New York: William Morrow, 1986), p. 470.
3. Ibid.
4. Szulc, p. 469;
   Georgie Anne Geyer, *Guerrilla Prince: The Untold Story of Fidel Castro* (Boston: Little, Brown, 1991), p. 206.
5. Szulc, pp. 468–469.
6. Ibid. p. 470.

Chapter Two

1. Jaime Suchlicki, *Cuba from Columbus to Castro* (New York: Brassey's, 1990), p. 3.
2. Szulc, pp. 95–96.
3. Ibid. p. 103.
4. Peter Bourne, *Fidel: A Biography of Fidel Castro* (New York: Dodd, Mead, 1986), p. 16.
5. Geyer, pp. 24–25.
6. Ibid. p. 34.

Chapter Three

1. Bourne, p. 21.
2. Szulc, p. 111.
3. Ibid. p. 112.
4. Ibid. p. 116.
5. Ibid. pp. 119–120.
6. Szulc, p. 92.
7. Suchlicki, pp. 78, 84.
8. Bourne, p. 28.

Chapter Four

1. Szulc, p. 153.
2. Ibid. p. 138.
3. Ibid. pp. 156–157.
4. Bourne, p. 54.
5. Geyer, p. 55.

Chapter Five

1. Bourne, p. 66.
2. Geyer, p. 105.
3. Ibid. p. 101.
4. Ibid. p. 125.
5. Szulc, pp. 296–297;
   Geyer, p. 129;
   Sebastian Balfour, *Castro* (New York: Longman, 1990), p. 41.

Chapter Six

1. Bourne, p. 94;
   Geyer, p. 133.
2. Bourne, p. 103.
3. Ibid. p. 115.
4. Balfour, p. 48.
5. Bourne, p. 148.
6. Ibid. pp. 154–155.

Chapter Seven

1. Bourne, p. 166.
2. Ibid. p. 174.
3. Ibid. p. 197.
4. Ibid. p. 211.
5. Geyer, pp. 262–263.
6. Bourne, p. 222.
7. Balfour, p. 71.

Chapter Eight

1. Balfour, p. 80.
2. Ibid. p. 72.
3. Bourne, p. 239.
4. Ibid.
5. Balfour, p. 84.
6. Bourne, pp. 265–266.
7. Balfour, p. 79.
8. Ibid. p. 91.
9. Ibid. p. 93.
10. Ibid. p. 97.
11. Ibid. pp. 98–99.

Chapter Nine

1. Suchlicki, p. 185.
2. Bourne, p. 283.
3. Ibid. p. 124.
4. Ibid. p. 129.

Chapter Ten

1. Balfour, p. 133–134.
2. Geyer, p. 367;
   Bourne, p. 295.
3. Balfour, p. 136.
4. Ibid. p. 140.
5. Ibid. p. 141.

6. Geyer, p. 381.
7. Rodman D. Griffin, *CQ Researcher*, November 29, 1991, p. 899.
8. Balfour, p. 153.
9. Ibid. p. 156.

Chapter Eleven

1. Griffin, p. 902.
2. Ibid. p. 899.
3. Ibid. p. 915.
4. Ibid. p. 899.
5. Spencer Reiss, *Newsweek*, August 10, 1992, p. 42.
6. *The New York Times*, July 29, 1992.
7. Griffin, p. 900.
8. Cathy Booth, *Time*, October 26, 1992, p. 56.
9. Griffin, p. 900.
10. Ibid. p. 901.
11. Ibid.

Bibliography

Balfour, Sebastian. *Castro.* New York: Longman, 1990.

Bentley, Judith. *Fidel Castro of Cuba.* New York: J. Messner, 1991 (young adults).

Bourne, Peter G. *Fidel: A Biography of Fidel Castro.* New York: Dodd, Mead & Co., 1986.

Geyer, Georgie Anne. *Guerrilla Prince: The Untold Story of Fidel Castro.* Boston: Little, Brown & Co., 1991.

Oppenheimer, Andres. *Castro's Final Hour.* New York: Simon and Schuster, 1992.

Suchlicki, Jaime. *Cuba from Columbus to Castro.* New York: Brassey's (US), Inc., 1990.

Szulc, Tad. *Fidel: A Critical Portrait.* New York: William Morrow & Co., 1986.

Vail, John. *Fidel Castro.* New York: Chelsea House, 1986 (young adults).

Index